CAMBRIDGE LIBRARY COLLECTION

Books of enduring scholarly value

Spiritualism and Esoteric Knowledge

Magic, superstition, the occult sciences and esoteric knowledge appear regularly in the history of ideas alongside more established academic disciplines such as philosophy, natural history and theology. Particularly fascinating are periods of rapid scientific advances such as the Renaissance or the nineteenth century which also see a burgeoning of interest in the paranormal among the educated elite. This series provides primary texts and secondary sources for social historians and cultural anthropologists working in these areas, and all who wish for a wider understanding of the diverse intellectual and spiritual movements that formed a backdrop to the academic and political achievements of their day. It ranges from works on Babylonian and Jewish magic in the ancient world, through studies of sixteenth-century topics such as Cornelius Agrippa and the rapid spread of Rosicrucianism, to nineteenth-century publications by Sir Walter Scott and Sir Arthur Conan Doyle. Subjects include astrology, mesmerism, spiritualism, theosophy, clairvoyance, and ghost-seeing, as described both by their adherents and by sceptics.

Researches in the Phenomena of Spiritualism

Published in 1874, this collection of reports by the chemist and scientific journalist Sir William Crookes (1832–1919) describes his controversial research into psychic forces. In 1870, Crookes decided that science had a duty to study preternatural phenomena associated with spiritualism, and he spent the next four years carrying out experiments which tested famous mediums including D. D. Home, Kate Fox and Florence Cook. This fascinating work describes Crookes' witnessing of the movement of bodies at a distance, rappings, changes in the weights of bodies, levitation of individuals and automatic writing. Although he was strongly criticised by his contemporaries, Crookes would not be deterred from his psychical research, demonstrating that he thought all natural phenomena worthy of scientific investigation. A great experimentalist, Crookes refused to be bound by tradition and convention, and his story reveals one of the important episodes in the history of the spiritualist movement.

Cambridge University Press has long been a pioneer in the reissuing of out-of-print titles from its own backlist, producing digital reprints of books that are still sought after by scholars and students but could not be reprinted economically using traditional technology. The Cambridge Library Collection extends this activity to a wider range of books which are still of importance to researchers and professionals, either for the source material they contain, or as landmarks in the history of their academic discipline.

Drawing from the world-renowned collections in the Cambridge University Library and other partner libraries, and guided by the advice of experts in each subject area, Cambridge University Press is using state-of-the-art scanning machines in its own Printing House to capture the content of each book selected for inclusion. The files are processed to give a consistently clear, crisp image, and the books finished to the high quality standard for which the Press is recognised around the world. The latest print-on-demand technology ensures that the books will remain available indefinitely, and that orders for single or multiple copies can quickly be supplied.

The Cambridge Library Collection brings back to life books of enduring scholarly value (including out-of-copyright works originally issued by other publishers) across a wide range of disciplines in the humanities and social sciences and in science and technology.

Researches in the Phenomena of Spiritualism

WILLIAM CROOKES

CAMBRIDGE
UNIVERSITY PRESS

CAMBRIDGE UNIVERSITY PRESS

Cambridge, New York, Melbourne, Madrid, Cape Town,
Singapore, São Paolo, Delhi, Mexico City

Published in the United States of America by Cambridge University Press, New York

www.cambridge.org
Information on this title: www.cambridge.org/9781108044134

© in this compilation Cambridge University Press 2012

This edition first published 1874
This digitally printed version 2012

ISBN 978-1-108-04413-4 Paperback

RESEARCHES

IN THE

PHENOMENA OF SPIRITUALISM.

BY WILLIAM CROOKES, F.R.S., &c.

PART I.

SPIRITUALISM VIEWED BY THE LIGHT OF MODERN SCIENCE, AND EXPERIMENTAL INVESTIGATIONS ON PSYCHIC FORCE,

WITH 16 ILLUSTRATIONS AND DIAGRAMS.

PRICE ONE SHILLING.

LONDON:

J. BURNS, 15 SOUTHAMPTON ROW, W.C.

H. NISBET, PRINTER, 219 GEORGE STREET, GLASGOW.

REPRINTED FROM THE QUARTERLY JOURNAL OF SCIENCE.

RESEARCHES

IN THE

PHENOMENA OF SPIRITUALISM.

BY WILLIAM CROOKES, F.R.S., &c.

In One Volume, Handsome Cloth, price 5s.

This Work is also Published in Three Parts, price One Shilling each.

PART I.

SPIRITUALISM

VIEWED BY THE LIGHT OF MODERN SCIENCE,

AND

EXPERIMENTAL INVESTIGATIONS ON PSYCHIC FORCE,

With 16 Illustrations and Diagrams. Price 1s.

PART II.

PSYCHIC FORCE AND MODERN SPIRITUALISM,

A REPLY TO THE *Quarterly Review* AND OTHER CRITICS,

To which is added Correspondence upon Dr. Carpenter's Asserted Refutation of the Author's Experimental Proof of the Existence of a hitherto Undetected Force.

With Two Illustrations. Price 1s.

PART III.

NOTES OF AN INQUIRY.

INTO THE

PHENOMENA CALLED SPIRITUAL,

DURING THE YEARS 1870-73.

To which are added Three Letters, entitled " Miss Florence Cook's Mediumship," " Spirit-Forms," and " The Last of Katie King ; the Photographing of Katie King by the aid of the Electric Light."

Price 1s.

LONDON:

J. BURNS, 15 SOUTHAMPTON ROW, HOLBORN, W.C.

RESEARCHES

IN

THE PHENOMENA

OF

SPIRITUALISM.

BY

WILLIAM CROOKES, F.R.S.

[*Reprinted from* THE QUARTERLY JOURNAL OF SCIENCE.]

LONDON:

J. BURNS, 15 SOUTHAMPTON ROW, HOLBORN, W.C.

1874.

GLASGOW:
H. NISBET, PRINTER AND STEREOTYPER,
219 GEORGE STREET.

SPIRITUALISM

LIGHT OF MODERN SCIENCE.

SOME weeks ago the fact that I was engaged in investigating Spiritualism, so called, was announced in a contemporary:* and in consequence of the many communications I have since received, I think it desirable to say a little concerning the investigation which I have commenced. Views or opinions I cannot be said to possess on a subject which I do not pretend to understand. I consider it the duty of scientific men who have learnt exact modes of working, to examine phenomena which attract the attention of the public, in order to confirm their genuineness, or to explain, if possible, the delusions of the honest and to expose the tricks of deceivers. But I think it a pity that any public announcement of a man's investigation should be made until he has shown himself willing to speak out.

A man may be a true scientific man, and yet agree with Professor De Morgan, when he says—"I have both seen and heard, in a manner which would make unbelief impossible, things called spiritual, which cannot be taken by a rational being to be capable of explanation by imposture, coincidence, or mistake. So far I feel the ground firm under me; but when it comes to what is the cause of these phenomena, I find I cannot adopt any explanation which has yet been suggested. . . . The physical explanations which I have seen are easy, but miserably insufficient. The spiritual hypothesis is sufficient, but ponderously difficult."

Regarding the sufficiency of the explanation, I am not able to speak. That certain physical phenomena, such as the movement of material substances, and the production of sounds resembling electric discharges, occur under cir-

* *The Athenæum.*

cumstances in which they cannot be explained by any
physical law at present known, is a fact of which I am as
certain as I am of the most elementary fact in chemistry.
My whole scientific education has been one long lesson in
exactness of observation, and I wish it to be distinctly
understood that this firm conviction is the result of most
careful investigation.   But I cannot, at present, hazard even
the most vague hypothesis as to the cause of the phenomena.   Hitherto I have seen nothing to convince me of the
truth of the "spiritual" theory.   In such an inquiry the
intellect demands that the spiritual proof must be absolutely incapable of being explained away; it must be so
strikingly and convincingly true that we cannot, dare not
deny it.

Faraday says, "Before we proceed to consider any question involving physical principles, we should set out with
clear ideas of the naturally possible and impossible."   But
this appears like reasoning in a circle: we are to investigate
nothing till we know it to be *possible*, whilst we cannot say
what is *impossible*, outside pure mathematics, till we know
everything.

In the present case I prefer to enter upon the enquiry
with no preconceived notions whatever as to what can or
cannot be, but with all my senses alert and ready to convey
information to the brain; believing, as I do, that we have
by no means exhausted all human knowledge or fathomed
the depths of all the physical forces, and remembering that
the great philosopher already quoted said, in reference to
some speculations on the gravitating force, "Nothing is too
wonderful to be true, if it be consistent with the laws of
nature; and in such things as these, experiment is the best
test of such consistency."

The modes of reasoning of scientific men appear to be
generally misunderstood by spiritualists with whom I have
conversed, and the reluctance of the trained scientific mind
to investigate this subject is frequently ascribed to unworthy
motives.   I think, therefore, it will be of service if I here
illustrate the modes of thought current amongst those who
investigate science, and say what kind of experimental
proof science has a right to demand before admitting a new
department of knowledge into her ranks.   We must not
mix up the exact and the inexact.   The supremacy of
accuracy must be absolute.

The first requisite is to be sure of facts; then to ascertain
conditions; next, laws.   Accuracy and knowledge of detail
stand foremost amongst the great aims of modern scientific

men. No observations are of much use to the student of science unless they are truthful and made under test conditions; and here I find the great mass of spiritualistic evidence to fail. In a subject which, perhaps, more than any other lends itself to trickery and deception, the precautions against fraud appear to have been, in most cases, totally insufficient, owing, it would seem, to an erroneous idea that to ask for such safeguards was to imply a suspicion of the honesty of some one present. We may use our own unaided senses, but when we ask for instrumental means to increase their sharpness, certainty, and trustworthiness under circumstances of excitement and difficulty, and when one's natural senses are liable to be thrown off their balance, offence is taken.

In the countless number of recorded observations I have read, there appear to be few instances of meetings held for the express purpose of getting the phenomena under test conditions, in the presence of persons properly qualified by scientific training to weigh and adjust the value of the evidence which might present itself. The only good series of test experiments I have met with were tried by the Count de Gasparin, and he, whilst admitting the genuineness of the phenomena, came to the conclusion that they were not due to supernatural agency.

The pseudo-scientific spiritualist professes to know everything: no calculations trouble his serenity, no hard experiments, no long laborious readings; no weary attempts to make clear in words that which has rejoiced the heart and elevated the mind. He talks glibly of all sciences and arts, overwhelming the enquirer with terms like "electro-biologize," "psychologize," "animal magnetism," &c.—a mere play upon words, showing ignorance rather than understanding. Popular science such as this is little able to guide discovery rushing onwards to an unknown future; and the real workers of science must be extremely careful not to allow the reins to get into unfit and incompetent hands.

In investigations which so completely baffle the ordinary observer, the thorough scientific man has a great advantage. He has followed science from the beginning through a long line of learning, and he knows, therefore, in what direction it is leading; he knows that there are dangers on one side, uncertainties on another, and almost absolute certainty on a third: he sees to a certain extent in advance. But, where every step is towards the marvellous and unexpected, precautions and tests should be multiplied rather than diminished. Investigators must work; although their work may be very small in quantity if only compensation be made by its intrinsic excellence. But, even in this realm of marvels,—this wonder-land towards which scientific enquiry is sending out its pioneers,—can anything be more astonishing than the delicacy of the instrumental aids which the workers bring with them to supplement the observations of their natural senses?

The spiritualist tells of bodies weighing 50 or 100 lbs. being lifted up into the air without the intervention of any known force; but the scientific chemist is accustomed to use a balance which will render sensible a weight so small that it would take ten thousand of them to weigh one grain; he is, therefore, justified in asking that a power, professing to be guided by intelligence, which will toss a heavy body up to the ceiling, shall also cause his delicately-poised balance to move under test conditions.

The spiritualist tells of tapping sounds which are produced in different parts of a room when two or more persons sit quietly round a table. The scientific experimenter is entitled to ask that these taps shall be produced on the stretched membrane of his phonautograph.

The spiritualist tells of rooms and houses being shaken, even to injury, by superhuman power. The man of science merely asks for a pendulum to be set vibrating when it is in a glass case and supported on solid masonry.

The spiritualist tells of heavy articles of furniture moving from one room to another without human agency. But the man of science has made instruments which will divide an inch into a million parts; and he is justified in doubting the accuracy of the former observations, if the same force is powerless to move the index of his instrument one poor degree.

The spiritualist tells of flowers with the fresh dew on them, of fruit, and living objects being carried through closed windows, and even solid brick-walls. The scientific investigator naturally asks that an additional weight (if it be only the 1000th part of a grain) be deposited on one pan of his balance when the case is locked. And the chemist asks for the 1000th of a grain of arsenic to be carried through the sides of a glass tube in which pure water is hermetically sealed.

The spiritualist tells of manifestations of power, which would be equivalent to many thousands of "foot-pounds," taking place without known agency. The man of science, believing firmly in the conservation of force, and that it is never produced without a corresponding exhaustion of something to replace it, asks for some such exhibitions of power to be manifested in his laboratory, where he can weigh, measure, and submit it to proper tests.*

For these reasons and with these feelings I began an inquiry suggested to me by eminent men exercising great influence on the thought of the country. At first, like other men who thought little of the matter and saw little, I believed that the whole affair was a superstition, or at least an unexplained trick. Even at this moment I meet with cases which I cannot *prove* to be anything else; and in some cases I am sure that it is a delusion of the senses.

I by no means promise to enter fully into this subject; it seems very difficult to obtain opportunities, and numerous failures certainly may dishearten anyone. The persons in whose presence these phenomena take place are few in number, and opportunities for experimenting with previously arranged apparatus are rarer still. I should feel it to be a great satisfaction if I could bring out light in any direction, and I may safely say that I care not in what direction. With this end in view, I appeal to any of my readers who may possess a key to these strange phenomena, to further the progress of the truth by assisting me in my investigations. That the subject has to do with strange physiological conditions is clear, and these in a sense may be called "spiritual" when they produce certain results in our minds. At present the phenomena I have observed baffle explanation; so do the phenomena of thought, which are also spiritual, and which no philosopher has yet understood. No man, however, denies them.

The explanations given to me, both orally and in most of the books I have read, are shrouded in such an affected ponderosity of style, such an attempt at disguising poverty of ideas in grandiloquent language, that I feel it impossible, after driving off the frothy diluent, to discern a crystalline residue of meaning. I confess that the reasoning of some spiritualists would almost seem to justify Faraday's severe statement—that many dogs have the power of coming to much more logical conclusions. Their speculations utterly ignore all theories of force being only a form of molecular motion, and they speak of Force, Matter, and Spirit, as

* In justice to my subject, I must state that, on repeating these views to some of the leading "spiritualists" and most trustworthy "mediums" in England, they express perfect confidence in the success of the enquiry, if honestly carried out in the spirit here exemplified; and they have offered to assist me to the utmost of their ability, by placing their peculiar powers at my disposal. As far as I have proceeded, I may as well add that the preliminary tests have been satisfactory.

three distinct entities, each capable of existing without the others; although they sometimes admit that they are mutually convertible.

These spiritualists are certainly not much in advance of an alchemical writer, who says—

> " I asked Philosophy how I should
> Have of her the thing I would.
> She answered me when I was able
> To make the water malliable,
> Or else the way if I could finde,
> To measure out a yard of winde ;
> Then shalt thou have thine own desire,
> When thou canst weigh an ounce of Fire ;
> Unless that thou canst do these three,
> Content thyselfe, thou get'st not me."

It has been my wish to show that science is gradually making its followers the representatives of care and accuracy. It is a fine quality that of uttering undeniable truth. Let, then, that position not be lowered, but let words suit facts with an accuracy equal to that with which the facts themselves can be ascertained ; and in a subject encrusted with credulity and superstition, let it be shown that there *is* a class of facts to be found upon which reliance can be placed, so far, that we may be certain they will never change. In common affairs a mistake may have but a short life, but in the study of nature an imperfect observation may cause infinite trouble to thousands. The increased employment of scientific methods will promote exact observation and greater love of truth among enquirers, and will produce a race of observers who will drive the worthless residuum of spiritualism hence into the unknown limbo of magic and necromancy.

If spiritualists would but attend to the teachings of their own prophets, they would no longer have to complain of the hostile attitude of Science ; for hear what Thomas L. Harris urges, in his " Lyric of a Golden Age !"

> " The nearer to the practical men keep—
> The less they deal in vague and abstract things
> The less they deal in huge mysterious words—
> The mightier is their power.
>
> .   .   .
>
> The simplest peasant who observes a truth,
> And from a fact deduces principle,
> Adds solid treasure to the public wealth.
> The theorist, who dreams a rainbow dream,
> And calls hypothesis philosophy,
> At best is but a paper financier,
> Who palms his specious promises for gold.
> Facts are the basis of philosophy ;
> Philosophy the harmony of facts
> Seen in their right relation.

[From the "Quarterly Journal of Science," July 1, 1871.]

EXPERIMENTAL INVESTIGATION OF A NEW FORCE.

TWELVE months ago in this journal* I wrote an article, in which, after expressing in the most emphatic manner my belief in the occurrence, under certain circumstances, of phenomena inexplicable by any known natural laws, I indicated several tests which men of science had a right to demand before giving credence to the genuineness of these phenomena. Among the tests pointed out were, that a "delicately poised balance should be moved under test conditions;" and that some exhibition of power equivalent to so many "foot-pounds" should be "manifested in his laboratory, where the experimentalist could weigh, measure, and submit it to proper tests." I said, too, that I could not promise to enter fully into this subject, owing to the difficulties of obtaining opportunities, and the numerous failures attending the enquiry; moreover, that "the persons in whose presence these phenomena take place are few in number, and opportunities for experimenting with previously arranged apparatus are rarer still."

Opportunities having since offered for pursuing the investigation, I have gladly availed myself of them for applying to these phenomena careful scientific testing experiments, and I have thus arrived at certain definite results which I think it right should be published. These experiments appear conclusively to establish the existence of a new force, in some unknown manner connected with the human organisation, which for convenience may be called the Psychic Force.

Of all the persons endowed with a powerful development of this Psychic Force, and who have been termed "mediums" upon quite another theory of its origin, Mr. Daniel Dunglas Home is the most remarkable, and it is mainly owing to

* See Quarterly Journal of Science, vol. vii., p. 316, July, 1870.

the many opportunities I have had of carrying on my investigation in his presence that I am enabled to affirm so conclusively the existence of this Force. The experiments I have tried have been very numerous, but owing to our imperfect knowledge of the conditions which favour or oppose the manifestations of this force, to the apparently capricious manner in which it is exerted, and to the fact that Mr. Home himself is subject to unaccountable ebbs and flows of the force, it has but seldom happened that a result obtained on one occasion could be subsequently confirmed and tested with apparatus specially contrived for the purpose.

Among the remarkable phenomena which occur under Mr. Home's influence, the most striking, as well as the most easily tested with scientific accuracy, are—(1) the alteration in the weight of bodies, and (2) the playing of tunes upon musical instruments (generally an accordion, for convenience of portability) without direct human intervention, under conditions rendering contact or connection with the keys impossible. Not until I had witnessed these facts some half-dozen times, and scrutinised them with all the critical acumen I possess, did I become convinced of their objective reality. Still, desiring to place the matter beyond the shadow of doubt, I invited Mr. Home on several occasions to come to my own house, where, in the presence of a few scientific enquirers, these phenomena could be submitted to crucial experiments.

The meetings took place in the evening, in a large room lighted by gas. The apparatus prepared for the purpose of testing the movements of the accordion, consisted of a cage, formed of two wooden hoops, respectively 1 foot 10 inches and 2 feet diameter, connected together by 12 narrow laths, each 1 foot 10 inches long, so as to form a drum-shaped frame, open at the top and bottom; round this 50 yards of insulated copper wire were wound in 24 rounds, each being rather less than an inch from its neighbour. These horizontal strands of wire were then netted together firmly with string, so as to form meshes rather less than 2 inches long by 1 inch high. The height of this cage was such that it would just slip under my dining table, but be too close to the top to allow of the hand being introduced into the interior, or to admit of a foot being pushed underneath it. In another room were two Grove's cells, wires being led from them into the dining-room for connection, if desirable, with the wire surrounding the cage.

The accordion was a new one, having been purchased by

myself for the purpose of these experiments at Wheatstone's, in Conduit Street. Mr. Home had neither handled nor seen the instrument before the commencement of the test experiments.

In another part of the room an apparatus was fitted up for experimenting on the alteration in the weight of a body. It consisted of a mahogany board, 36 inches long by 9½ inches wide and 1 inch thick. At each end a strip of mahogany 1½ inches wide was screwed on, forming feet. One end of the board rested on a firm table, whilst the other end was supported by a spring balance hanging from a substantial tripod stand. The balance was fitted with a self-registering index, in such a manner that it would record the maximum weight indicated by the pointer. The apparatus was adjusted so that the mahogany board was horizontal, its foot resting flat on the support. In this position its weight was 3 lbs., as marked by the pointer of the balance.

Before Mr. Home entered the room, the apparatus had been arranged in position, and he had not even the object of some parts of it explained before sitting down. It may, perhaps, be worth while to add, for the purpose of anticipating some critical remarks which are likely to be made, that in the afternoon I called for Mr. Home at his apartments, and when there he suggested that, as he had to change his dress, perhaps I should not object to continue our conversation in his bedroom. I am, therefore, enabled to state positively, that no machinery, apparatus, or contrivance of any sort was secreted about his person.

The investigators present on the test occasion were an eminent physicist, high in the ranks of the Royal Society, whom I will call Dr. A. B.; a well-known Serjeant-at-Law, whom I will call Serjeant C. D.; my brother; and my chemical assistant.*

Mr. Home sat in a low easy chair at the side of the table. In front of him under the table was the aforesaid cage, one of his legs being on each side of it. I sat close to him on his left, and another observer sat close to him on his right, the rest of the party being seated at convenient distances round the table.

* It argues ill for the boasted freedom of opinion among scientific men, that they have so long refused to institute a scientific investigation into the existence and nature of facts asserted by so many competent and credible witnesses, and which they are freely invited to examine when and where they please. For my own part, I too much value the pursuit of truth, and the discovery of any new fact in nature, to avoid enquiry because it appears to clash with prevailing opinions. But as I have no right to assume that others are equally willing to do this, I refrain from mentioning the names of my friends without their permission.

For the greater part of the evening, particularly when anything of importance was proceeding, the observers on each
side of Mr. Home kept their feet respectively on his feet,
so as to be able to detect his slightest movement.

The temperature of the room varied from 68° to 70° F.

Mr. Home took the accordion between the thumb and
middle finger of one hand at the opposite end to the
keys (see woodcut, Fig. 1), (to save repetition this will
be subsequently called "in the usual manner.") Having

FIG. 1.

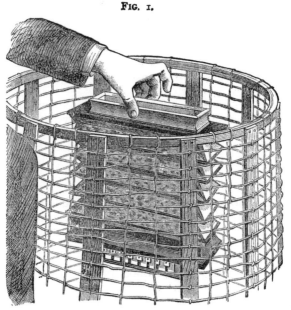

previously opened the bass key myself, and the cage being
drawn from under the table so as just to allow the accordion
to be passed in with its keys downwards, it was pushed back
as close as Mr. Home's arm would permit, but without hiding
his hand from those next to him (see Fig. 2). Very soon
the accordion was seen by those on each side to be waving
about in a somewhat curious manner; then sounds came
from it, and finally several notes were played in succession. Whilst this was going on, my assistant went under
the table, and reported that the accordion was expanding
and contracting; at the same time it was seen that the
hand of Mr. Home by which it was held was quite still, his
other hand resting on the table.

Presently the accordion was seen by those on either side of Mr. Home to move about, oscillating and going round and round the cage, and playing at the same time. Dr. A. B. now looked under the table, and said that Mr. Home's hand appeared quite still whilst the accordion was moving about emitting distinct sounds.

Mr. Home still holding the accordion in the usual manner in the cage, his feet being held by those next him, and his other hand resting on the table, we heard distinct and separate notes sounded in succession, and then a simple air

FIG. 2.

was played. As such a result could only have been produced by the various keys of the instrument being acted upon in harmonious succession, this was considered by those present to be a crucial experiment. But the sequel was still more striking, for Mr. Home then removed his hand altogether from the accordion, taking it quite out of the cage, and placed it in the hand of the person next to him. The instrument then continued to play, no person touching it and no hand being near it.

I was now desirous of trying what would be the effect of passing the battery current round the insulated wire of the cage, and my assistant accordingly made the connection with the wires from the two Grove's cells. Mr. Home again held the instrument inside the cage in the same manner as before, when it immediately sounded and moved about vigorously. But whether the electric current passing round the cage assisted the manifestation of force inside, it is impossible to say.

The accordion was now again taken without any visible touch from Mr. Home's hand, which he removed from it entirely and placed upon the table, where it was taken by the person next to him, and seen, as now were both his hands, by all present. I and two of the others present saw the accordion distinctly floating about inside the cage with no visible support. This was repeated a second time, after a short interval. Mr. Home presently re-inserted his hand in the cage and again took hold of the accordion. It then commenced to play, at first chords and runs, and afterwards a well-known sweet and plaintive melody, which it executed perfectly in a very beautiful manner. Whilst this tune was being played, I grasped Mr. Home's arm, below the elbow, and gently slid my hand down it until I touched the top of the accordion. He was not moving a muscle. His other hand was on the table, visible to all, and his feet were under the feet of those next to him.

Having met with such striking results in the experiments with the accordion in the cage, we turned to the balance apparatus already described. Mr. Home placed the tips of his fingers lightly on the extreme end of the mahogany board which was resting on the support, whilst Dr. A. B. and myself sat, one on each side of it, watching for any effect which might be produced. Almost immediately the pointer of the balance was seen to descend. After a few seconds it rose again. This movement was repeated several times, as if by successive waves of the Psychic Force. The end of the board was observed to oscillate slowly up and down during the experiment.

Mr. Home now of his own accord took a small hand-bell and a little card match-box, which happened to be near, and placed one under each hand, to satisfy us, as he said, that he was not producing the downward pressure (see Fig. 3). The very slow oscillation of the spring balance became more marked, and Dr. A. B., watching the index, said that he saw it descend to 6½ lbs. The normal weight of the board as so suspended being 3 lbs., the additional downward pull was therefore 3½ lbs. On looking immediately afterwards at the automatic register, we saw that the index had at one time descended as low as 9 lbs., showing a maximum pull of 6 lbs. upon a board whose normal weight was 3 lbs.

In order to see whether it was possible to produce much effect on the spring balance by pressure at the place where Mr. Home's fingers had been, I stepped upon the table and stood on one foot at the end of the board. Dr. A. B., who was observing the index of the balance, said that the whole weight of my body (140 lbs.) so applied only sunk the index 1½ lbs., or 2 lbs. when I jerked up and down. Mr. Home had been sitting in a low easy-chair, and could not, therefore, had he tried his utmost, have exerted any material influence on these results. I need scarcely add that his feet as well as his hands were closely guarded by all in the room.

This experiment appears to me more striking, if possible, than the one with the accordion. As will be seen on referring to the cut (Fig. 3), the board was arranged perfectly horizontally, and it was particularly noticed that Mr.

FIG. 3.

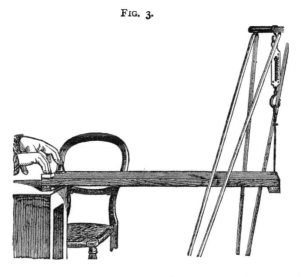

Home's fingers were not at any time advanced more than 1½ inches from the extreme end, as shown by a pencil-mark, which, with Dr. A. B.'s acquiescence, I made at the time. Now, the wooden foot being also 1½ inches wide, and resting flat on the table, it is evident that no amount of pressure exerted within this space of 1½ inches could produce any action on the balance. Again, it is also evident that when the end furthest from Mr. Home sank, the board would turn on the further edge of this foot as on a fulcrum. The arrangement was consequently that of a see-saw, 36 inches in length, the fulcrum being 1½ inches from one end; were he therefore to have exerted a downward pressure, it would have been in opposition to the force which was causing the other end of the board to move down.

The slight downward pressure shown by the balance when I stood on the board was owing probably to my foot extending beyond this fulcrum.

I have now given a plain unvarnished statement of the facts from copious notes written at the time the occurrences were taking place, and copied out in full immediately after. Indeed, it would be fatal to the object I have in view—that of urging the scientific investigation of these phenomena—were I to exaggerate ever so little; for although to my readers Dr. A. B. is at present represented by incorporeal initials, to me the letters represent a power in the scientific world that would certainly convict me if I were to prove an untrustworthy narrator.

I confess I am surprised and pained at the timidity or apathy shown by scientific men in reference to this subject. Some little time ago, when an opportunity for examination was first presented to me, I invited the co-operation of some scientific friends in a systematic investigation; but I soon found that to obtain a scientific committee for the investigation of this class of facts was out of the question, and that I must be content to rely on my own endeavours, aided by the co-operation from time to time of a few scientific and learned friends who were willing to join in the inquiry. I still feel that it would be better were such a committee of known men to be formed, who would meet Mr. Home in a fair and unbiased manner, and I would gladly assist in its formation; but the difficulties in the way are great.

A committee of scientific men met Mr. Home some months ago at St. Petersburg. They had one meeting only, which was attended with negative results; and on the strength of this they published a report highly unfavourable to Mr. Home. The explanation of this failure, *which is all they have accused him of*, appears to me quite simple. Whatever the nature of Mr. Home's power, it is very variable, and at times entirely absent. It is obvious that the Russian experiment was tried when the force was at a minimum. The same thing has frequently happened within my own experience. A party of scientific men met Mr. Home at my house, and the results were as negative as those at St. Petersburg. Instead, however, of throwing up the inquiry we patiently repeated the trial a second and a third time, when we met with results which were positive.

These conclusions have not been arrived at hastily or on insufficient evidence. Although space will allow only the publication of the details of one trial, it must be clearly understood that for some time past I have been making similar experiments and with like results. The meeting on the occasion here described was for the purpose of confirming previous observations by the application of crucial tests, with carefully arranged apparatus, and in the presence of irreproachable witnesses.

Respecting the cause of these phenomena, the nature of the force to which, to avoid periphrasis, I have ventured to give the name of *Psychic*, and the correlation existing between that and the other forces of nature, it would be wrong to hazard the most vague hypothesis. Indeed, in enquiries connected so intimately with rare physiological and psychological conditions, it is the duty of the enquirer to abstain altogether from framing theories until he has accumulated a sufficient number of facts to form a substantial basis upon which to reason. In the presence of strange phenomena as yet unexplored and unexplained following each other in such rapid succession, I confess it is difficult to avoid clothing their record in language of a sensational character. But, to be successful, an inquiry of this kind must be undertaken by the philosopher without prejudice and without sentiment. Romantic and superstitious ideas should be entirely banished, and the steps of his investigation should be guided by intellect as cold and passionless as the instruments he uses. Having once satisfied himself that he is on the track of a new truth, that single object should animate him to pursue it, without regarding whether the facts wich occur before his eyes are "naturally possible or impossible."

Since this article was in type, the Author has been favoured with the following letters from Dr. Huggins and Mr. Sergeant Cox—the Dr. A. B. and Sergeant C. D. therein referred to:—

Upper Tulse Hill, S.W.,
June 9, 1871.

DEAR MR. CROOKES,—Your proof appears to me to contain a correct statement of what took place in my presence at your house. My position at the table did not permit me to

B

be a witness to the withdrawal of Mr. Home's hand from the accordion, but such was stated to be the case at the time by yourself and by the person sitting on the other side of Mr. Home.

The experiments appear to me to show the importance of further investigation, but I wish it to be understood that I express no opinion as to the cause of the phenomena which took place.   Yours very truly,

WILLIAM HUGGINS.

WM. CROOKES, Esq, F.R.S.

36, Russell Square,
June 8, 1871.

MY DEAR SIR,—Having been present, for the purpose of scrutiny, at the trial of the experiments reported in this paper, I readily bear my testimony to the perfect accuracy of your description of them, and to the care and caution with which the various crucial tests were applied.

The results appear to me conclusively to establish the important fact, that there is a force proceeding from the nerve-system capable of imparting motion and weight to solid bodies within the sphere of its influence.

I noticed that the force was exhibited in tremulous pulsations, and not in the form of steady continuous pressure, the indicator rising and falling incessantly throughout the experiment. This fact seems to me of great significance, as tending to confirm the opinion that assigns its source to the nerve organisation, and it goes far to establish Dr. Richardson's important discovery of a nerve atmosphere of various intensity enveloping the human structure.

Your experiments completely confirm the conclusion at which the Investigation Committee of the Dialectical Society arrived, after more than forty meetings for trial and test.

Allow me to add that I can find no evidence even tending to prove that this force is other than a force proceeding from, or directly dependent upon, the human organisation, and therefore, like all other forces of nature, wholly within the province of that strictly scientific investigation to which you have been the first to subject it.

Psychology is a branch of science as yet almost entirely unexplored, and to the neglect of it is probably to be attributed the seemingly strange fact that the existence of this nerve-force should have remained so long untested, unexamined, and almost unrecognised.

Now that it is proved by mechanical tests to be a fact in nature (and if a fact, it is impossible to exaggerate its importance to physiology and the light it must throw upon the obscure laws of life, of mind and the science of medicine) it cannot fail to command the immediate and most earnest examination and discussion by physiologists and by all who take an interest in that knowledge of "man," which has been truly termed "the noblest study of mankind." To avoid the appearance of any foregone conclusion, I would recommend the adoption for it of some appropriate name, and I venture to suggest that the force be termed the *Psychic Force;* the persons in whom it is manifested in extraordinary power *Psychics;* and the science relating to it *Psychism* as, being a branch of *Psychology*.

Permit me, also, to propose the early formation of a *Psychological Society*, purposely for the promotion, by means of experiment, papers, and discussion, of the study of that hitherto neglected Science.—I am, &c.,

EDWD. WM. COX.

To W. CROOKES, Esq., F.R.S.

[From the "Quarterly Journal of Science," October 1, 1871.]

SOME FURTHER EXPERIMENTS ON PSYCHIC FORCE.

"I am attacked by two very opposite sects—the scientists and the know-nothings. Both laugh at me—calling me 'the frogs' dancing master.' Yet I know that I have discovered one of the greatest forces in nature."—GALVANI.

IT was my intention to have allowed a longer time to elapse before again writing on the subject of "Psychic Force" in this journal. My reason for this resolve was not so much owing to want of new matter and fresh results,—on the contrary, I have much that is new in the way of experimental evidence in support of my previous conclusions,—but I felt some reluctance to impose on the readers of the "Quarterly Journal of Science" a subject which they might view with little favour. When the editor of a scientific journal is also an experimental investigator, or a student of any special branch of knowledge, there is a natural tendency on his part to unduly exalt the importance of that which is occupying his thoughts at the time; and thus the journal which he conducts is in danger of losing breadth of basis, of becoming the advocate of certain opinions, or of being coloured by special modes of thought.

The manner in which the experimental investigation described in the last "Quarterly Journal" has been received, removes any doubt I might entertain on this score. The very numerous communications which have been addressed to the office of this journal show that another paper on the same subject will not be distasteful to a large number of those who did me the honour to read my former article; whilst it appears to be generally assumed that I should take an early opportunity to reply to some of the criticisms provoked by the remarkable character of the experimental results which I described.

Many of the objections made to my former experiments are answered by the series about to be related. Most of the criticisms to which I have been subjected have been perfectly fair and courteous, and these I shall endeavour to meet in the fullest possible manner. Some critics, however, have fallen into the error of regarding me as an advocate for certain *opinions*, which they choose to ascribe to me, though in truth my single purpose has been to state fairly and to offer no opinion. Having evolved men of straw from their own imagination, they proceed vigorously to slay them,

under the impression that they are annihilating me. Others,
—and I am glad to say they are very few,—have gone
so far as to question my veracity:—"Mr. Crookes must
get better witnesses before he can be believed!" Accustomed
as I am to have my word believed without witnesses, this is
an argument which I cannot condescend to answer. All
who know me and read my articles will, I hope, take it
for granted that the *facts* I lay before them are correct, and
that the experiments were honestly performed, with the
single object of eliciting *the truth.*

It is edifying to compare some of the present criticisms
with those that were written twelve months ago. When I
first stated in this journal that I was about to investigate
the phenomena of so-called spiritualism, the announcement
called forth universal expressions of approval. One said
that my "statements deserved respectful consideration;"
another, expressed "profound satisfaction that the subject
was about to be investigated by a man so thoroughly qualified as," &c.; a third was "gratified to learn that the
matter is now receiving the attention of cool and clear-
headed men of recognised position in science;" a fourth asserted that no one could doubt Mr. Crookes's ability to
conduct the investigation with rigid philosophical imparti-
ality;" and a fifth was good enough to tell its readers that
"if men like Mr. Crookes grapple with the subject, taking
nothing for granted until it is proved, we shall soon know
how much to believe."

These remarks, however, were written too hastily. It was
taken for granted by the writers that the results of my experiments would be in accordance with their preconceptions.
What they really desired was not *the truth,* but an additional
witness in favour of their own foregone conclusion. When
they found that the facts which that investigation established
could not be made to fit those opinions, why,—"so much
the worse for the facts." They try to creep out of their
own confident recommendations of the enquiry by declaring
that "Mr. Home is a clever conjurer, who has duped us all."
"Mr. Crookes might, with equal propriety, examine the per-
formances of an Indian juggler." "Mr. Crookes must get
better witnesses before he can be believed." "The thing is
too absurd to be treated seriously." "It is impossible, and
therefore can't be."* "The observers have all been biologised (!) and fancy they saw things occur which really never
took place," &c., &c.

---

* The quotation occurs to me—"I never said it was possible, I only said it
was true."

These remarks imply a curious oblivion of the very functions which the scientific enquirer has to fulfil. I am scarcely surprised when the objectors say that I have been deceived merely because they are unconvinced without personal investigation, since the same unscientific course of *à priori* argument has been opposed to all great discoveries. When I am told that what I describe cannot be explained in accordance with preconceived ideas of the laws of nature, the objector really begs the very question at issue and resorts to a mode of reasoning which brings science to a standstill. The argument runs in a vicious circle: we must not assert a fact till we know that it is in accordance with the laws of nature, while our only knowledge of the laws of nature must be based on an extensive observation of facts. If a new fact seems to oppose what is called a law of nature, it does not prove the asserted fact to be false, but only that we have not yet ascertained all the laws of nature, or not learned them correctly.

In his opening address before the British Association at Edinburgh this year, Sir William Thomson said, " Science is bound by the everlasting law of honour to face fearlessly every problem which can fairly be presented to it." My object in thus placing on record the results of a very remarkable series of experiments is to present such a problem, which, according to Sir William Thomson, " Science is bound by the everlasting law of honour to face fearlessly." It will not do merely to deny its existence, or try to sneer it down. Remember, I hazard no hypothesis or theory whatever; I merely vouch for certain facts, my only object being—the *truth*. Doubt, but do not deny; point out, by the severest criticism, what are considered fallacies in my experimental tests, and suggest more conclusive trials; but do not let us hastily call our senses lying witnesses merely because they testify against preconceptions. I say to my critics, Try the experiments; investigate with care and patience as I have done. If, having examined, you discover imposture or delusion, proclaim it and say how it was done. But, if you find it be a fact, avow it fearlessly, as " by the everlasting law of honour " you are bound to do.

I may at once answer one objection which has been made in several quarters, viz., that my results would carry more weight had they been tried a greater number of times, and with other persons besides Mr. Home. The fact is, I have been working at the subject for two years, and have found nine or ten different persons who possess psychic power in more or less degree ; but its development in Mr. D. D. Home is so powerful, that, having satisfied myself by careful experiments that the phenomena observed were genuine, I have, merely as a matter of convenience, carried on my experiments with him, in preference to working with others in whom the power existed in a less striking degree. Most of the experiments I am about to describe, however, have been tried with another person other than Mr. Home, and in his absence.

Before proceeding to relate my new experiments, I desire to say a few words respecting those already described. The objection has been raised that announcements of such magnitude should not be made on the strength of one or two experiments hastily performed. I reply that the conclusions were not arrived at hastily, nor on the results of two or three experiments only. In my former paper ("Quarterly Journal of Science," page 340), I remarked :—"Not until I had witnossed these facts some half-dozen times, and scrutinised them with all the critical acumen I possess, did I become convinced of their objective reality." Before fitting up special apparatus for these experiments, I had seen on five separate occasions, objects varying in weight from 25 to 100 lbs., temporarily influenced in such a manner, that I, and others present could with difficulty lift them from the floor Wishing to ascertain whether this was a physical fact, or merely due to a variation in the power of our own strength under the influence of imagination, I tested with a weighing machine the phenomenon on two subsequent occasions when I had an opportunity of meeting Mr. Home at the house of a friend. On the first occasion, the increase of weight was from 8 lbs. normally, to 36 lbs., 48 lbs., and 46 lbs., in three successive experiments tried under strict scrutiny. On the second occasion, tried about a fortnight after, in the presence of other observers, I found the increase of weight to be from 8 lbs. to 23 lbs., 43 lbs., and 27 lbs., in three successive trials, varying the conditions. As I had the entire management of the above-mentioned experimental trials, employed an instrument of great accuracy, and took every care to exclude the possibility of the results being influenced by trickery, I was not unprepared for a satisfactory result when the fact was properly tested in my own laboratory. The meeting on the occasion formerly described was, therefore, for the purpose of confirming my previous observations by the application of crucial tests, with carefully arranged apparatus of a still more delicate nature.

That this is a legitimate subject for scientific inquiry scarcely needs assertion. Faraday himself did not consider it beneath his dignity to examine similar phenomena; and, in a letter to Sir Emerson Tennent, written in 1861 on the occasion of a proposed experimental inquiry all into the phenomena occurring in Mr. Home's presence, he wrote:—" Is he (Mr. Home) willing to investigate as a philosopher, and, as such, to have no concealments, no darkness, to be open in communication, and to aid inquiry all that he can ? . . . Does he consider the effects natural or supernatural? If they be the glimpses of natural action not yet reduced to law, ought it not to be the duty of every-one who has the least influence in such actions personally to develope them, and to aid others in their development, by the utmost openness and assistance, and by the application of every critical method, either mental or experimental, which the mind of man can devise?"

If circumstances had not prevented Faraday from meeting Mr. Home, I have no doubt he would have witnessed phenomena similar to those I am about to describe, and he could not have failed to see that they offered "glimpses of natural action not yet reduced to law."

I have already alluded to the publication of the ill-success encountered by the members of the St. Petersburg Committee. Had the results been satisfactory, it must be fairly assumed that the members would have been equally ready to publish a report of their success.

I am informed by my friend Professor Boutlerow,* that during the last winter, he tried almost the same experiments as those here detailed, and with still more striking results. The normal tension on the dynamometer being 100 lbs., it was increased to about 150 lbs., Mr. Home's hands being placed in contact with the apparatus in such a manner that any exertion of power on his part would diminish, instead of increase, the tension.

In 1854, Count Agenor de Gasparin published a book,† giving full details of a large series of physical experiments which he had tried with some private friends in whom this force was found to be strongly developed. His experiments were very numerous and were carried on under the strictest test conditions. The fact of motion of heavy bodies without mechanical contact was demonstrated over and over

* Professor of Chemistry at the University of St. Petersburg ; author of a work on Chemistry, entitled " Lehrbuch der Organischen Chemie ;" Leipzig 1868.

† Science *versus* Spiritualism. Paris, 1854. New York, 1857.

again. Careful experiments were made to measure the force both of gravitation and of levitation thus communicated to the substances under trial, and an ingenious plan was adopted by which Count de Gasparin was enabled to obtain a rough numerical estimate of the power of the psychic force in each individual. The author finally arrived at the conclusion that all these phenomena are to be accounted for by the action of natural causes, and do not require the supposition of miracles nor the intervention of spirits or diabolical influences. He considers it as a fact fully established by his experiments, that the will, in certain states of the organism, can act at a distance on inert matter, and most of his work is devoted to ascertaining the laws and conditions under which this action manifests itself.

In 1855, M. Thury, a Professor at the Academy of Geneva, published a work,* in which he passed in review Count de Gasparin's experiments, and entered into full details of researches he had been simultaneously carrying on. Here, also, the trials were made with private friends, and were conducted with all the care which a scientific man could bring to bear on the subject. Space will not allow me to quote the valuable numerical results obtained by M. Thury, but from the following headings of some of his chapters, it will be seen that the enquiry was not conducted superficially:—Facts which Establish the Reality of the New Phenomenon; Mechanical Action rendered Impossible; Movements effected without Contact; The Causes ; Conditions requisite for the Production and Action of the Force; Conditions for the Action with Respect to the Operators; The Will; Is a Plurality of Operators Necessary? Preliminary Requisites; Mental Condition of the Operators; Meteorological Conditions; Conditions with Respect to the Instruments Operated upon; Conditions relative to the Mode of Action of the Operators on the Instruments; Action of Substances interposed; Production and Transmission of the Force; Examination of the Assigned Causes; Fraud; Unconscious Muscular Action produced in a particular Nervous State; Electricity; Nervo-magnetism; M. de Gasparin's Theory of a Special Fluid; General Question as to the Action of Mind on Matter. 1st Proposition; In the ordinary conditions of the body the will only acts directly within the sphere of the organism. 2nd Proposition ; Within the organism itself there are a series of mediate acts. 3rd Proposition: The substance on which the mind

---

* Geneva; Librairie Allemande de J. Kessmann. 1855.

acts directly—the *psychode*—is only susceptible of very simple modification under the influence of the mind; Explanations which are based on the Intervention of Spirits. M. Thury refutes all these explanations, and considers the effects due to a peculiar substance, fluid, or agent, pervading, in a manner similar to the luminiferous ether of the scientist, all matter, nervous, organic, or inorganic—which he terms *psychode*. He enters into full discussion as to the properties of this state or form of matter, and proposes the term *ectenic force* (ἐκτένια, extension), for the power exerted when the mind acts at a distance through the influence of the psychode.*

There is likewise another case on record in which similar test experiments were tried, with like results, by a thoroughly competent observer. The late Dr. Robert Hare, in one of his works,† gives an engraving of an apparatus very similar to my own, by which the young man with whom he was experimenting was prevented from having any other communication with the apparatus except through water; yet, under these circumstances, the spring balance indicated the exertion of a force equal to 18 lbs. The details of this experiment were communicated by Dr. Hare, to the American Association for the Advancement of Science, at the meeting in August, 1855.

The references I now give afford an answer to the statement that these results must be verified by others. They have been verified over and over again. Indeed, my own experiments may be regarded merely as verifications of results already obtained and published by eminent scientific men in this and other countries.‡

But I was not content with this. I felt that having the opportunity of showing these phenomena to others, I might

---

* Professor Thury's ectenic and my psychic force are evidently equivalent terms. Had I seen his work three months ago I should have adopted his term. The suggestion of a similar hypothetical nervous fluid has now reached us from another and totally different source, expounded with distinct views, and couched in the language of one of the most important professions—I allude to the theory of a nervous atmosphere advanced by Dr. Benjamin W. Richardson, M.D., F.R.S., in the "Medical Times," No. 1088, May 6, 1871.

† "Experimental Investigation;" By Robert Hare, M.D., Emeritus Professor of Chemistry in the University of Pennsylvania, &c. New York: Partridge and Britton, 1858.

‡ The Report of the Dialectical Society on Spiritualism will appear in a few days, and it will be seen that the Investigation Committee, though commencing their experiments with the entire conviction that they should expose an imposture, have ended by affirming that they are convinced of the existence of a force emanating from the human organisation, by which motion may be imparted to heavy substances, and audible sounds made on solid bodies without muscular contact; they also state that this force is often directed by some intelligence.

at a future time be blamed did I not, once for all, take the very best means of bringing them before the notice of the scientific world. Accordingly I forwarded an account of my experiments to the Royal Society on June 15, 1871, and addressed myself to the two secretaries of the Royal Society, Professor Sharpey and Professor Stokes, inviting them to my house to meet Mr. Home, at the same time asking them to be prepared for negative results, and to come a second, or, if necessary, a third time, before forming a judgment.

Dr. Sharpey politely declined the invitation.

Professor Stokes replied that he thought there was a fallacy in my apparatus, and concluded by saying—

"The facts you mentioned in the paper were certainly at first sight very strange, but still possible modes of explanation occurred to me which were not precluded by what I read in the paper. If I have time when I go to London I will endeavour to call at your house. I don't want to meet anyone; my object being to scrutinise the apparatus, not to witness the effects."

To this I replied on June 20th; the following extracts are taken from my answer:—

" I am now fitting up apparatus in which contact is made through water only, in such a way that transmission of mechanical movement to the board is impossible; and I am also arranging an experiment in which Mr. Home will not touch the apparatus at all. This will only work when the power is very strong; but last night I tried an experiment of this kind, and obtained a considerable increase of tension on the spring balance when Mr. Home's hands were three inches off. With him the power is so great that I can work with large and crude materials, and measure the force in pounds. But I propose to make a delicate apparatus, with a mirror and reflected ray of light, to show fractions of grains. Then I hope to find this force is not confined to a few, but is, like the magnetic state, universal. The subject shall have a 'most scrupulously searching physical scrutiny,' and whatever results I obtain shall be published. I consider it my duty to send first to the Royal Society, for by so doing I deliberately stake my reputation on the truth of what I send. But will the Society (or the Committee*) accept my facts as facts, or will they require vouchers for my integrity? If my statements of fact are taken as correct, and only my interpretation or arrangements of apparatus objected to, then it would seem to be right to give me an opportunity of answering these objections before finally deciding. The other supposition—that my facts are incorrect—I cannot admit the discussion of till I am definitely assured that such is entertained.

"Mr. Home is coming here on Wednesday and Friday evenings: if you can come on either or both occasions at 8 p.m., I shall be glad to see you, or if you only wish to scrutinise the apparatus, I will be here at any time you like to name."

On the 28th of June another paper was sent to the Royal Society. Two days after, Professor Stokes wrote a letter, from which I quote:—

" As I was otherwise engaged so as not to be able conveniently to go to your house, I may as well mention the possible sources of error which occurred to me with reference to your first apparatus. I don't suppose they all exist;

---

* Alluding to a rumoured rejection of my paper by the Committee of the Royal Society.

but it is evidently, as you yourself would freely admit, for the *assertor* of a new force to remove all sources of reasonable objection.

"The breadth of the foot of the board was, I think, $1\frac{1}{2}$ or 2 inches, and the bell placed on it was, perhaps, 2 or 3 inches broad. (I can't carry the exact figures in my head.) Join the left edge* of the top of the bell, *a*, with the right hand edge, *b*, of the base of the bell, and let *e f* be the joining line. Then we may suppose the fingers to have pressed in any direction short of the limiting line *e f*. Also as the board was rigid, the fulcrum for aught we know may have been at *c*. From *c* let fall a perpendicular *c m* on the line *e f*. Then the pressure of the finger may have acted at the distance, *c m*, from the fulcrum. Also, as the base lay flat on the table and both were rigid, for aught we know, an infinitesimal, and therefore imperceptible, tilt communicated to the table at the time of trying the experiment may have shifted the fulcrum from the edge *d* to the edge *c*, so that the weight of the hand may have acted by an arm longer than before by *c d*, which would have contributed to the result.

"In your second paper the uncertainty as to the broad bearing is removed. But when the hand was dipped into the water the pressure on the base of the glass vessel (after a little time if the connecting hole be narrow) is increased by the weight of the water displaced, and that would of course depress the balance.

"I don't think much of mere tremors, for it would require very elaborate appliances to prove that they were not due to a passing train or omnibus or to a tremor in the body of one of the company. . . . . What do you wish to be done with the papers !"

To this I replied as follows, on July 1st:—

"In your letter of the 30th ult., just received, you are quite right in saying that I would freely admit that 'the *assertor* of a new force should remove all sources of reasonable objection.' In your previous letter of the 19th of June, you write with equal fairness, that 'your opinion is that you (the R. S.) ought not to refuse to admit evidence of the existence of a hitherto unsuspected

FIG. I (half scale).

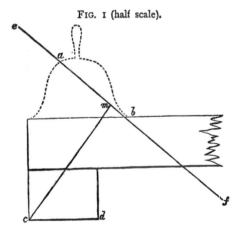

force; but that before printing anything on such a subject, you ought to require a most scrupulously searching physical scrutiny of the evidence adduced in favour of the existence of such a force.'

---

* The diagram referred to here is shown, drawn to scale, in my answer further on. The experiment under discussion is the one figured and described in the last number of the "Quarterly Journal of Science," page 345.

" You have now been good enough to explain to me in detail what the fallacy is which you think exists in my first experiments, and what you consider to be the possible sources of error in my subsequent trials.

" On re-drawing the diagram you give in your letter, Fig. 1, to the full size, supplying the deficient data, viz., the position of the shoulder, *a*, and the point, *b*, your line *c m* appears to be about 2·9 inches long ; and, as you assume that the fulcrum shall be at *c*, the lever becomes one of the third order, the two forces acting respectively at *p*=2·9 inches, and at *q*=36 inches from *c*. What power, P, must be exerted at *p* to overcome a resistance or weight, Q, of 6 lbs. at the end of the lever, *q* ?

$$P p = Q q.$$
Hence, $P + 2 \cdot 9 = Q + 36.$
$$\therefore P = 74 \cdot 5 \text{ lbs.}$$

Therefore, it would have required a force of 74·5 lbs. to have been exerted by Mr. Home to have produced the results, even if all your suppositions are granted ; and, considering that he was sitting in a low easy chair, and four pairs of sharp, suspicious eyes were watching to see that he exerted no force at all, but kept the tips of his fingers lightly on the instrument, it is sufficiently evident that an exertion of this pressure was impossible. A few pounds vertical pressure was all he could have effected.

" Again, you are not justified in assuming that the fulcrum was at *c*. Granting that ' an infinitesimal and therefore imperceptible tilt ' might, at the very first movement, have thrown it from *d* to *c*, it is evident that the movement would at once throw it forward again from *c* to *d*. To have failed to have done so, the tilt must have been so obvious as to have been detected at once.

" But, as I said in my last paper, I prefer to appeal to new experiments rather than argue about old ones, and hence my employment of the water for transmitting the force. The depth of water in the copper hemisphere was only 1½ inches, whilst the glass vessel was 9 inches in diameter.* I have just tried the experiment of immersing my hand to the very utmost in the copper vessel (Mr. Home only dipped in the tips of his fingers) and the rise of the level of the water is not sufficient to produce any movement whatever on the index of the balance, the friction of the apparatus being enough to absorb the ounce or two thus added to the weight. In my more delicate apparatus, this increase of hydrostatic pressure produces a decided movement of the spot of light, but this difficulty I shall overcome by placing the water vessel over the fulcrum, or on the short side of it.

" You say ' you don't think much of mere tremors,' as if in the other experiments described in my second paper the movements of the apparatus were only of this kind. This is not the case ; the quivering of the apparatus always took place before the index moved, and the upward and downward motion of the board and index was of a very slow and deliberate character, occupying several seconds for each rise and fall; a tremor produced by passing vehicles is a very different thing from a steady vertical pull of from 4 to 8 lbs., lasting for several seconds.

" You say the session is now over, and ask what I wish to be done with the papers.

" Three years ago (June 27th, 1868), I sent a paper to the Society, ' On the Measurement of the Luminous Intensity of Light,' just after the session closed. It was not read till December 17th. My *wish* would be for a similar course to be adopted in the present instance, although I am scarcely sanguine enough to expect that so much notice will be taken of these communications. So many scientific men are now examining into these strange phenomena (including many Fellows of the Society), that it cannot be many years before the subject will be brought before the scientific world in a way that will enforce attention. I confess that, in sending in these papers to the Society, I have been actuated more by the desire of being the first scientific experimenter

---

* For a description of this apparatus, see p. 484.

who has ventured to take such a course, than by any particular desire that they should meet with immediate attention. I owe to the Society the first intimation of important scientific results, and these I shall continue to send, '*pour prendre date,*' if for no other reason."

"The Spectator" of July 22nd contained an editorial note, in which it is asserted that my paper was declined by the committee:—

"The Royal Society, they say, was quite open to communications advocating the existence of a force in nature as yet unknown, if such communications contained scientific evidence adequate to establish its probability; but that, looking to the inherent improbability of the case as stated by Mr. Crookes, and the *entire want of scientific precision* in the evidence adduced by him, the paper was not regarded as one deserving the attention of the Royal Society."

This paragraph not only states that my papers were declined, but proceeds to state the grounds of their rejection. The fact is, that a quorum of the committee of papers not having been present, the question was deferred to the next session in November, and on inquiry at Burlington House, I am informed by the Assistant-Secretary of the Royal Society that my papers, with others, are still awaiting the decision of the committee. Consequently the statement of a rejection was not only premature, but purely imaginary.

It appears, however, that there were some grounds for this statement, for in "The Spectator" of July 29th, 1871, the editor replies as follows:—

"Our note was not founded on any mere rumour. The words we used contained an exact copy of the words conveyed to us as used, not, as we inadvertently stated by the committee, but by one of the secretaries, Professor Stokes, who in the absence of a quorum, exercised *pro tempore* the usual discretionary authority in regard to papers offered."

I am unable to explain how it is that Professor Stokes's statements to me and to the editor of "The Spectator" bear so different an interpretation, or why a weekly newspaper was chosen for first conveying to me a decision of the committee of papers of the Royal Society.

At the urgent request of gentlemen on the committee of section A, I communicated a paper consisting of about sixteen closely-written pages to the British Association, in which I recounted some of the experiments described in the present paper. Section A referred the paper to a committee to decide whether it should be read. Professor Stokes afterwards handed to me the following document:—

"*Report on Mr. Crookes's Paper.*"

August 7, 1871.

"The paper having been placed in my hands about ten o'clock, and a decision wanted in writing by a quarter to eleven, I have been obliged to be hasty.

"The subject *seems to be investigated in a philosophical spirit,* and I do not see the explanation of the result of the first class of experiments, while at the same time I am not prepared to give in my adhesion without a thorough sifting by more individuals than one. I don't see much use discussing the thing in the sections, crowded as we already are; but if a small number of persons in whom the public would feel confidence choose to volunteer to act as members of a committee for investigating the subject, I don't see any objection to appointing such committee. I have heard too much of the tricks of Spiritualists to make me willing to give my time to such a committee myself.

"G. G. STOKES."

Whilst I cannot but regret that a physicist of such eminence as Professor Stokes should "be hasty," in deciding on the merits of a paper which it is physically impossible he could have even once read through, I am glad to find that he no longer continues to speak of the "entire want of scientific precision in the evidence adduced" by me, but rather admits that "the subject seems to be investigated in a philosophical spirit."

In submitting these experiments, it will not seem strange that I should consider them final until rebutted by arguments also drawn from facts, and that I should seek to know on what grounds contra-statements are founded. Professor Allen Thomson, at the recent meeting of the British Association, remarked that no course of inquiry into the matter before us "can deserve the name of study or investigation." And why not? On the other hand, Professor Challis, of Cambridge, writes, "In short, the testimony has been so abundant and consentaneous, that either the facts must be admitted to be such as are reported, or the possibility of certifying facts by human testimony must be given up." It is certainly not too much to suppose that Dr. Thomson had some grounds for his statement; and, indeed, "I have," he owns, "been fully convinced of this (the fallacies of spiritualistic demonstration) by repeated examinations;" but where are the results of his investigations to be found? They must be very conclusive to warrant him in the use of such expressions as "a few men of acknowledged reputation in some departments of science have surrendered their judgments to these foolish dreams, *otherwise* appearing to be within the bounds of sanity." If Dr. Thomson's dogmatic denial arises from the mere strangeness of the facts I have set forth, what can he think of the address of the President for this year. Surely the conception of a nerve-force is no more difficult than that "of the inner mechanism of the atom;" and again, any investigation, be it worthy the name or not, bearing on a matter in which eminent men have avowed their belief, which takes a leading rank among the social questions of the day, and which numbers its adherents by millions, is surely as full of merit, and as instructive to all, as hypothetical inquiries into "interatomic atmospheres" and "gyrating interatomic atoms." Professor Huxley has observed, "If there is one thing clear about the progress of modern science, it is the tendency to reduce all scientific problems, except those that are purely mathematical, to problems in molecular physics—that is to say, to attractions, repulsions, motions, and co-ordination of the ultimate particles of matter! Yet these ultimate particles, molecules, or atoms, are creatures of the imagination, and as pure assumptions as the spirits of the spiritualist." But perhaps Dr. Allen Thomson's respect for mathematics is so great that he is blind to actuality. It does not speak well for modern scientific philosophy that, after the startling revelations of the spectroscope during the last decade, investigations should be scouted because they pertain to an ulterior state of things of which at present we have little idea. That I have furnished no dynamic equivalent of psychic force, or given no formulæ for the variable intensity of Mr. Home's power, is certainly no argument whatever against the existence of such a force. Men thought before the syllogism was invented, and, strange as it may seem to some minds, force existed before its demonstration in mathematical formulæ.

As an answer to Professor Balfour Stewart's rather bold conjecture, that Mr. Home possesses great electro-biological power (whatever that may mean), by which he influences those present, I point to the curves illustrating this paper ; however susceptible the *persons* in the room might have been to that assumed influence, it will hardly be contended that Mr. Home biologised the recording instruments.

I will not occupy more time with personal matters, or with explanations forced from me in self-defence against uncourteous commentaries based on unjust misrepresentations ; but I will proceed to describe the experiments, most of which, I may remark, might have been witnessed by Professor Stokes and Professor Sharpey, had they accepted the invitations I gave them.

On trying these experiments for the first time, I thought that actual contact between Mr. Home's hands and the suspended body whose weight was to be altered was essential to the exhibition of the force ; but I found afterwards that this was not a necessary condition, and I therefore arranged my apparatus in the following manner :—

The accompanying cuts (Figs. 2, 3, 4) explain the arrangement. Fig. 2 is a general view, and Figs. 3 and 4 show the essential parts more in detail. The reference letters are the same in each illustration. A B is a mahogany board, 36 inches long by 9½ inches wide, and 1 inch thick. It is suspended at the end, B, by a spring balance, C,

FIG. 2.

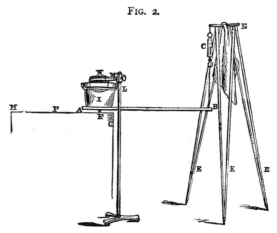

furnished with an automatic register, D. The balance is suspended from a very firm tripod support, E.

The following piece of apparatus is not shown in the figures. To the moving index, O, of the spring balance, a

FIG. 3

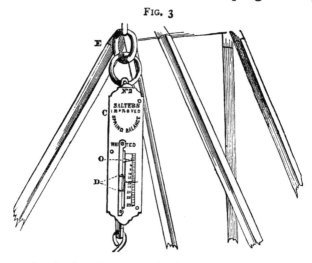

fine steel point is soldered, projecting horizontally outwards. In front of the balance, and firmly fastened to it, is a grooved frame carrying a flat box similar to the dark box of a photographic camera. This box is made to travel by clock-work horizontally in front of the moving index, and it contains a sheet of plate-glass which has been smoked over a flame. The projecting steel point impresses a mark on this smoked surface. If the balance is at rest, and the clock set going, the result is a perfectly straight horizontal line. If the clock is stopped and weights are placed on the

FIG. 4.

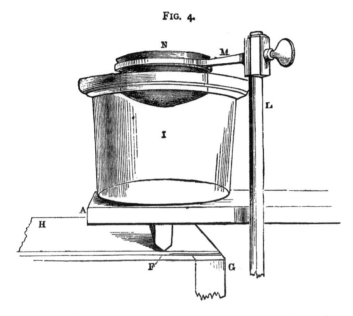

end B of the board, the result is a vertical line, whose length depends on the weight applied. If, whilst the clock draws the plate along, the weight of the board (or the tension on the balance) varies, the result is a curved line, from which the tension in grains at any moment during the continuance of the experiments can be calculated.

The instrument was capable of registering a diminution of the force of gravitation as well as an increase; registrations of such a diminution were frequently obtained. To avoid complication, however, I will only here refer to results in which an increase of gravitation was experienced.

The end B of the board being supported by the spring balance, the end A is supported on a wooden strip, F, screwed across its lower side and cut to a knife edge (see Fig. 4). This fulcrum rests on a firm and heavy wooden stand, G H. On the board, exactly over* the fulcrum, is placed a large glass vessel filled with water, I. L is a massive iron stand, furnished with an arm and a ring, M N, in which rests a hemispherical copper vessel perforated with several holes at the bottom.

The iron stand is 2 inches from the board A B, and the arm and copper vessel, M N, are so adjusted that the latter dips into the water $1\frac{1}{2}$ inches, being $5\frac{1}{2}$ inches from the bottom of I, and 2 inches from its circumference. Shaking or striking the arm M, or the vessel N, produces no appreciable mechanical effect on the board, A B, capable of affecting the balance. Dipping the hand to the fullest extent into the water in N does not produce the least appreciable action on the balance.

As the mechanical transmission of power is by this means entirely cut off between the copper vessel and the board A B, the power of muscular control is thereby completely eliminated.

For convenience I will divide the experiments into groups 1, 2, 3, &c., and I have selected one special instance in each to describe in detail. Nothing, however, is mentioned which has not been repeated more than once, and in some cases verified, in Mr. Home's absence, with another person possessing similar powers.

There was always ample light in the room where the experiments were conducted (my own dining-room) to see all that took place.

Experiment I.—The apparatus having been properly adjusted before Mr. Home entered the room, he was brought in, and asked to place his fingers in the water in the copper vessel, N. He stood up and dipped the tips of the fingers of his right hand in the water, his other hand and his feet being held. When he said he felt a power, force, or influence, proceeding from his hand, I set the clock going, and almost immediately the end B of the board was seen to descend slowly and remain down for about 10 seconds ; it then descended a little further, and afterwards rose to its normal height. It then descended again, rose suddenly, gradually sunk for 17 seconds, and finally rose to its normal height, where it remained till the experiment was concluded. The lowest point marked on the glass was equivalent to a direct pull of about 5000 grains. The accompanying figure (5) is a copy of the curve traced on the glass.

---

* In my first experiments with this apparatus, referred to in Professor Stokes's letter and my answer (page 479), the glass vessel was not quite over the fulcrum, but was nearer B.

Experiment II.—Contact through water having proved to be as effectual as actual mechanical contact, I wished to see if the power or force could affect the weight, either through other portions of the apparatus or through the air. The glass vessel and iron stand, &c., were therefore removed,

Fig. 5.

Scale of Seconds.

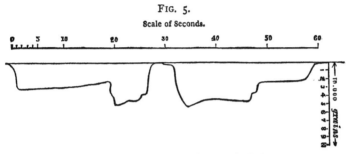

The horizontal scale of seconds shows the time occupied in the movements, the experiment lasting one minute. The vertical scale shows the tension in grains exerted on the balance at any moment.

as an unnecessary complication, and Mr. Home's hands were placed on the stand of the apparatus at P (Fig. 2). A gentleman present put his hand on Mr. Home's hands, and his foot on both Mr. Home's feet, and I also watched him closely all the time. At the proper moment the clock was

Fig. 6.

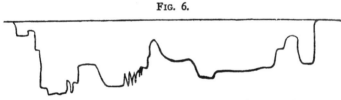

In this and the two following figures the scales, both vertical and horizontal, are the same as in Fig. 5.

again set going; the board descended and rose in an irregular manner, the result being a curved tracing on the glass, of which Fig. 6 is a copy.

Experiment III.—Mr. Home was now placed one foot from the board A B, on one side of it. His hands and feet

Fig. 7.

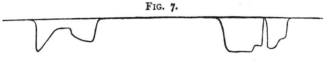

were firmly grasped by a bystander, and another tracing, of which Fig. 7 is a copy, was taken on the moving glass plate.

Experiment IV.—(Tried on an occasion when the power was stronger than on the previous occasions). **Mr.** Home was now placed 3 feet from the apparatus, his hands and feet being tightly held. The clock was set going when he gave the word, and the end B of the board soon descended, and again rose in an irregular manner, as shown in Fig. 8.

The following series of experiments were tried with more delicate apparatus, and with another person, a lady, Mr. Home being absent. As the lady is non-professional, I do

FIG. 8.

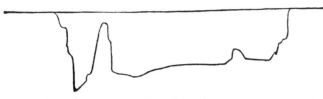

not mention **her** name. She has, however, consented to meet any scientific men whom I may introduce for purposes of investigation.

A piece of thin parchment, A, Figs. 9 and 10, is stretched tightly across a circular hoop of wood. B C is a light lever turning on D. At the end B is a vertical needle point touching the membrane A, and at C is another needle point, projecting

FIG. 9. (Plan.)

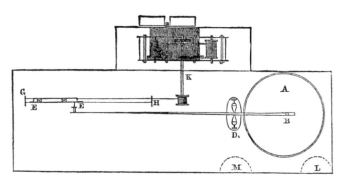

horizontally and touching a smoked glass plate, E F. This glass plate is drawn along in the direction H G by clockwork, K. The end B of the lever is weighted so that it shall quickly follow the movements of the centre of the disc, A. These movements are transmitted and recorded on the glass plate E F, by means of the lever and needle point C. Holes are cut in the side of the hoop to allow a free passage of air to the under side of the membrane. The apparatus was well tested beforehand by myself and others, to see that no shaking or jar on the table or support would interfere with the results : the line traced by the point C

FIG. 10. (Section.)

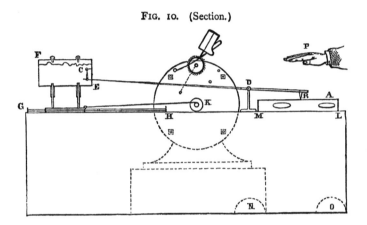

on the smoked glass was perfectly straight in spite of all our attempts to influence the lever by shaking the stand or stamping on the floor.

Experiment V.—Without having the object of the instrument explained to her, the lady was brought into the room and asked to place her fingers on the wooden stand at the points L M, Fig. 9. I then placed my hands over hers to enable me to detect any conscious or unconscious movement on her part. Presently percussive noises were heard on the parchment resembling the dropping of grains of sand on its surface. At each percussion a fragment of graphite which I had placed on the membrane was seen to be projected upwards about 1-50th of an inch, and the end C of the lever moved slightly up and down. Sometimes the sounds were as rapid as those from an induction-coil, whilst at others they were more than a second apart. Five or six tracings were taken, and in all cases a movement of the end C of the lever was seen to have occurred with each vibration of the membrane.

In some cases the lady's hands were not so near the membrane as L M, but were at N O, Fig. 10.

The accompanying Fig. 11 gives tracings taken from the plates used on these occasions.

Experiment VI.—Having met with these results in Mr. Home's absence, I was anxious to see what action would be produced on the instrument in his presence.

Accordingly I asked him to try, but without explaining the instrument to him.

FIG. 11.

Scale of Seconds.

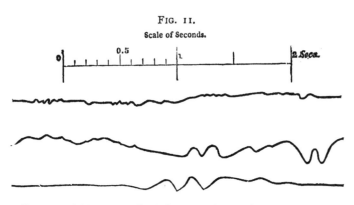

I grasped Mr. Home's right arm above the wrist and held his hand over the membrane, about 10 inches from its surface, in the position shown at p, Fig. 10. His other hand was held by a friend. After remaining in this position for about half a minute, Mr. Home said he felt some influence passing. I then set the clock going, and we all saw the index, c, moving up and down. The movements were much slower than in the former case, and were almost entirely unaccompanied by the percussive vibrations then noticed.

Figs. 12 and 13 show the curves produced on the glass on two of these occasions.

Figs. 11, 12, 13 are magnified.

These experiments *confirm beyond doubt* the conclusions at which I arrived in my former paper, namely, the existence of a force associated, in some manner not yet explained, with the human organisation, by which force, increased weight is capable of being imparted to solid bodies without physical contact. In the case of Mr. Home, the development of this force varies enormously, not only from week to week, but from hour to hour ; on some occasions the force is inappreciable by my tests for an hour or more, and then suddenly reappears in great strength. It is capable of acting at a distance from Mr. Home (not unfrequently as far as two or three feet), but is always strongest close to him.

Being firmly convinced that there could be no manifestation of one form of force without the corresponding expenditure of some other form of force, I for a long time searched in vain for evidence of any force or power being used up in the production of these results.

Now, however, having seen more of Mr. Home, I think I perceive what it is that this psychic force uses up for its development. In employing the terms *vital force*, or *nervous energy*, I am aware that I am employing words which convey very different significations to many investigators ; but after witnessing the painful state of nervous and bodily prostration in which some of these experiments have left

FIG. 12.

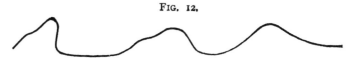

Mr. Home—after seeing him lying in an almost fainting condition on the floor, pale and speechless—I could scarcely doubt that the evolution of psychic force is accompanied by a corresponding drain on vital force.

I have ventured to give this new force the name of *Psychic Force*, because of its manifest relationship to certain psychological conditions, and because I was most desirous to avoid the foregone conclusions implied in the title under

FIG. 13.

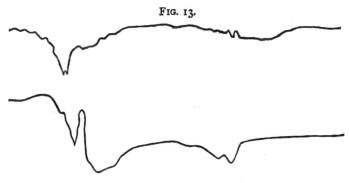

which it has hitherto been claimed as belonging to a province beyond the range of experiment and argument. But having found that it is within the province of purely scientific research, it is entitled to be known by a scientific name, and I do not think a more appropriate one could have been selected.

To witness exhibitions of this force it is not necessary to have access to known psychics. The force itself is probably possessed by all human beings, although the individuals endowed with an extraordinary amount of it are doubtless few. Within the last twelve months I have met in private families five or six persons possessing a sufficiently vigorous development to make me feel confident that similar results might be produced through their means to those here recorded, provided the experimentalist worked with more delicate apparatus, capable of indicating a fraction of a grain instead of recording pounds and ounces only.

As far as my other occupations will permit, I purpose to continue the experiments in various forms, and I will report from time to time their results. In the meanwhile I trust that others will be induced to pursue the investigation in its scientific form. It should, however, be understood that, equally with all other scientific experiments, these researches must be conducted in strict compliance with the conditions under which the force is developed. As it is an indispensable condition of experiments with frictional electricity that the atmosphere should be free from excess of moisture, and that no conducting medium should touch the instrument while the force is being generated, so certain conditions are found to be essential to the production and operation of the Psychic force, and unless these precautions are observed the experiments will fail. I am emphatic on this point, because unreasonable objections have sometimes been made to the Psychic Force that it is not developed under adverse conditions dictated by the experimentalist, who, nevertheless, would object to conditions being imposed upon himself in the exhibition of any of his own scientific results. But I may add, that the conditions required are very few, very reasonable, and in no way obstruct the most perfect observation and the application of the most rigid and accurate tests.

———————

Just before going to press I have received from my friend Professor Morton an advance sheet of the "Journal of the Franklin Institute," containing some remarks on my last paper by Mr. Coleman Sellers, a leading scientific engineer of the United States. The essence of his criticism is contained in the following quotation:—

"On page 341" (of the Quarterly Journal of Science) "we have given a mahogany board '36 inches long by 9½ inches wide, and 1 inch thick,' with 'at each end a strip of mahogany 1½ inches wide screwed on, forming feet.' This board was so placed as to rest with one end on the table, the other suspended by a spring balance, and, so suspended, it recorded a weight of 3 pounds ; *i.e.*, a *mahogany* board of the above dimensions is shown to weigh 6 pounds—3 pounds on the balance and 3 pounds on the table. A mechanic used to handling wood wonders how this may be. He looks through his limited library and finds that scientific men tell him that such a board should weigh about 13½ pounds. Did Mr. Crookes make this board himself? or did Mr. Home furnish it as one of his pieces of apparatus? . . . . It would have been more satisfactory if Mr. Crookes had stated, in regard to this board, who made it. . . . Let it be discovered that the 6 pound mahogany board was furnished by Mr. Home and the experiments will not be so convincing."

My experiments must indeed be convincing if so accomplished a mechanician as Mr. Coleman Sellers can find no worse fault with them than is expressed in the comments I have quoted. He writes in so matter-of-fact a manner, and deals so plausibly with dimensions and weights, that most persons would take it for granted that I really *had* committed the egregious blunder he points out.

Will it be believed, therefore, that my mahogany board does *weigh only 6 pounds?* Four separate balances in my own house tell me so, and my greengrocer confirms the fact.

It is easy to perceive into what errors a "mechanic" may fall when he relies for practical knowledge on his "limited library" instead of appealing to actual experiment.

I am sorry I cannot inform Mr. Sellers who made my mahogany board. It has been in my possession about sixteen years; it was originally cut off a length in a wood-yard; it became the stand of a spectrum camera, and as such is described with a cut in the "Journal of the Photographic Society" for January 21, 1856 (vol. ii., p. 293). It has since done temporary duty in the arrangement of various pieces of apparatus in my physical laboratory, and was selected for these particular experiments owing to its shape being more convenient than that of other available pieces of wood.

But is it seriously expected that I should answer such a question as "Did Mr. Home furnish the board?" Will not my critics give me credit for the possession of some amount of common sense? And can they not imagine that obvious precautions, which occur to them as soon as they sit down to pick holes in my experiments, are not unlikely to have also occurred to me in the course of prolonged and patient investigation?

The answer to this as to all other like objections is, Prove it to be an error by showing where the error lies, or, if a trick, by showing *how* the trick is performed. Try the experiment fully and fairly. If then fraud be found, expose it; if it be a truth, proclaim it. This is the only scientific procedure, and this it is that I purpose steadily to pursue.

RESEARCHES

IN THE

PHENOMENA OF SPIRITUALISM.

BY WILLIAM CROOKES, F.R.S., &c.

PART II.

PSYCHIC FORCE AND MODERN SPIRITUALISM:

A REPLY TO

THE *QUARTERLY REVIEW*, AND OTHER CRITICS,

TO WHICH IS ADDED

CORRESPONDENCE UPON DR CARPENTER'S ASSERTED RE-FUTATION OF THE AUTHOR'S EXPERIMENTAL PROOF OF THE EXISTENCE OF A HITHERTO UNDETECTED FORCE.

WITH TWO ILLUSTRATIONS.

PRICE ONE SHILLING.

LONDON:

J. BURNS, 15 SOUTHAMPTON ROW, W.C.

H. NISBET, PRINTER, 219 GEORGE STREET, GLASGOW.

REPRINTED FROM THE QUARTERLY JOURNAL OF SCIENCE.

RESEARCHES

IN THE

PHENOMENA OF SPIRITUALISM.

By WILLIAM CROOKES, F.R.S., &c.

In One Volume, Handsome Cloth, price 5s.

This Work is also Published in Three Parts, price One Shilling each.

PART I.

SPIRITUALISM

VIEWED BY THE LIGHT OF MODERN SCIENCE,

AND

EXPERIMENTAL INVESTIGATIONS ON PSYCHIC FORCE,

With 16 Illustrations and Diagrams.   Price 1s.

PART II.

PSYCHIC FORCE AND MODERN SPIRITUALISM,

A REPLY TO THE *Quarterly Review* AND OTHER CRITICS,

To which is added Correspondence upon Dr. Carpenter's Asserted Refutation of the Author's Experimental Proof of the Existence of a hitherto Undetected Force.

With Two Illustrations.   Price 1s.

PART III.

NOTES OF AN INQUIRY

INTO THE

PHENOMENA CALLED SPIRITUAL,

DURING THE YEARS 1870-73.

To which are added Three Letters, entitled " Miss Florence Cook's Mediumship," "Spirit-Forms," and "The Last of Katie King; the Photographing of Katie King by the aid of the Electric Light."

Price 1s.

LONDON:

J. BURNS, 15 SOUTHAMPTON ROW, HOLBORN, W.C.

PSYCHIC FORCE AND MODERN SPIRITUALISM:

A REPLY TO THE "QUARTERLY REVIEW."

[In presenting this article to the public, let me take the opportunity of explaining the exact position which I wish to occupy in respect to the subject of Psychic Force and Modern Spiritualism. I have desired to examine the phenomena from a point of view as strictly physical as their nature will permit. I wish to ascertain the laws governing the appearance of very remarkable phenomena which at the present time are occurring to an almost incredible extent. That a hitherto unrecognised form of Force—whether it be called psychic force or x force is of little consequence—is involved in this occurrence, is not with me a matter of opinion, but of absolute knowledge; but the nature of that force, or the cause which immediately excites its activity, forms a subject on which I do not at present feel competent to offer an opinion. I wish, at least for the present, to be considered in the position of an electrician at Valentia, examining by means of appropriate testing instruments, certain electrical currents and pulsations passing through the Atlantic cable; independently of their causation, and ignoring whether these phenomena are produced by imperfections in the testing instruments themselves—whether by earth currents or by faults in the insulation—or whether they are produced by an intelligent operator at the other end of the line.

WILLIAM CROOKES.

LONDON, *Dec.*, 1871.]

THE *Quarterly Review* for October contains an article under the title of "Spiritualism and its Recent Converts," in which my investigations and those of other scientific men are severely handled in the spiteful bad old style which formerly characterised this periodical, and which I thought had happily passed away. It has reverted to the unjustifiable fashion of testing truth by the character of individuals. Had the writer contented himself with fair criticism, however sharply administered, I should have taken no public notice of it, but have submitted with the best grace I could. But with reference to myself he has further mis-stated and distorted the aim and nature of my investigations, and written of me personally as confidently as if he had known me from boyhood and was thoroughly acquainted with every circumstance of my educational and scientific career, so that I feel constrained to protest against his manifest unfairness, prejudice, and incapacity to deal with the subject and my connection with it. Although other investigators, including Dr. Huggins, Serjeant Cox, Mr. Varley, and Lord Lindsay, are included in the indictment and found guilty with extenuating circumstances, for me he can feel no tenderness, which, were it not for my recent sins, he is good enough to observe he "might have otherwise felt for a man who has in his previous career made creditable use of his very limited opportunities." The other offenders who are attacked can well take care of themselves; let me now vindicate myself.

It was my good or evil fortune, as the case may be, to have an hour's conversation, if it may be so termed when the talking was all on one side, with the Quarterly Reviewer in question, when I had an opportunity of observing the curiously dogmatic tone of his mind and of estimating his incapacity to deal with any subject conflicting with his prejudices and prepossessions. At the last meeting of the British Association at Edinburgh we were introduced—he as a physiologist who had enquired into the matter fifteen or twenty years ago; I as a scientific investigator of a certain department of the subject; here is a sketch of our interview, accurate in substance if not identical in language.

"Ah! Mr. Crookes," said he, "I am glad I have an opportunity of speaking to you about this Spiritualism you have been writing about. You are only wasting your time. I devoted a great deal of time many years ago to mesmerism, clairvoyance, electro-biology, table-turning, spirit-rapping, and all the rest of it, and I found there was nothing in it. I explained it all in my article I wrote in the *Quarterly Review.* I think it a pity you have written anything on this subject before you made yourself intimately acquainted with my writings and my views on the subject. I have exhausted it."

"But, Sir," interposed I, "you will allow me to say you are mistaken, if—"

"No, no!" interrupted he, "I am not mistaken. I know what you would say. But it is quite evident from what you have just remarked, that you allowed yourself to be taken in by these people when you knew nothing whatever of the perseverance with which I and other competent men, eminently qualified to deal with the most difficult problems, had investigated these phenomena. You ought to have known that I explain everything you have seen by 'unconscious cerebration' and 'unconscious muscular action'; and if you had only a clear idea in your mind of the exact meaning of these two phrases, you would see that they are sufficient to account for everything."

"But, Sir—"

"Yes, yes; my explanations would clear away all the difficulties you have met with. I saw a great many mesmerists and clairvoyants, and it was all done by 'unconscious cerebration.' Whilst as to table-turning, everyone knows how Faraday put down that. It is a pity you were unacquainted with Faraday's beautiful indicator; but, of course, a person who knew nothing of my writings would not have known how he showed that unconscious muscular action was sufficient to explain all these movements."

"Pardon me," I interrupted, "but Faraday himself showed ——." But it was in vain, and on rolled the stream of unconscious egotism.

"Yes, of course; that is what I said. If you had known of Faraday's indicator and used it with Mr. Home, he would not have been able to go through his performance."

"But how," I contrived to ask, "could the indicator have served, seeing that neither Mr. Home nor anyone else touched the—"

"That's just it. You evidently know nothing of the indicator. You have not read my articles and explanations of all you saw, and you know nothing whatever of the previous history of the subject. Don't you think you have compromised the Royal Society? It is a great pity that you should be allowed there to revive subjects I put down ten years ago in my articles, and you ought not to be permitted to send papers in. However, we can deal with them." Here I was fain to keep silence. Meanwhile, my infallible interlocutor continued—

"Well, Mr. Crookes, I am very pleased I have had this opportunity of hearing these explanations from yourself. One learns so much in a conversation like this, and what you say has confirmed me on several points I was doubtful about before. Now, after I have had the benefit of hearing all about it from your own lips, I am more satisfied than ever that I have been always right, and that there is nothing in it but unconscious cerebration and muscular action."

At this juncture some good Samaritan turned the torrent of words on to himself; I thankfully escaped with a sigh of relief, and my memory recalled my first interview with Faraday, when we discussed table-turning and his contrivance to detect the part played by involuntary muscular effort in the production of that phenomenon. How different his courteous, kindly, candid demeanour towards me in similar circumstances compared with that of the Quarterly Reviewer!

Now, let me ask, what authority has the reviewer for designating me a recent convert to Spiritualism? Nothing that I have ever written can justify such an unfounded assumption. Indeed the dissatisfaction with which many spiritualists have received my articles clearly proves that they consider me unworthy of joining their fraternity. In my first published article the following sentences occur:—

> "Hitherto I have seen nothing to convince me of the 'spiritual' theory. In such an enquiry the intellect demands that the spiritual proof must be absolutely incapable of being explained away; it must be so strikingly and convincingly true that we cannot, dare not deny it."

> "Accuracy and knowledge of detail stand foremost amongst the great aims of modern scientific men. No observations are of much use to the student of science unless they are truthful and made under test conditions; and here I find the great mass of spiritualistic evidence to fail. In a subject which, perhaps, more than any other lends itself to trickery and deception, the precautions against fraud appear to have been, in most cases, totally insufficient."

> "I confess that the reasoning of some spiritualists would almost seem to justify Faraday's severe statement that many dogs have the power of coming to much more logical conclusions. Their speculations utterly ignore all theories of force being only a form of molecular motion, and they speak of Force, Matter, and Spirit as three distinct entities."

In a subsequent paper, I said that my experiments appeared to establish the existence of a new force connected, in some unknown manner, with the human organisation; but that it would be wrong to hazard the most vague hypothesis respecting the cause of the phenomena, the nature of this force, and the correlation existing between it and the other forces of nature. "Indeed," said I, "it is the duty of the enquirer to abstain altogether from framing theories until he has accumulated a sufficient number of facts to form a substantial basis upon which to reason." New forces must be found, or mankind must remain sadly ignorant of the mysteries of nature. We are unacquainted with a sufficient number of forces to do the work of the universe.

In a third paper, I brought forward many quotations from previous experimentalists, which showed that they did *not* ascribe the phenomena to Spiritualism. I then said that the name Psychic had been chosen for the subject "because I was most desirous to avoid the foregone conclusions implied in the title under which it has hitherto been claimed as belonging to a province beyond the range of experiment and argument."

Do these quotations look like Spiritualism? Does the train of thought running through them justify the Quarterly Reviewer in saying that "the lesson afforded by the truly scientific method followed by this great master of experimental philosophy (Faraday) . . . should not have been lost upon those who profess to be his disciples. But it has been entirely disregarded . . . by men from whom better things might have been expected"?

I have devoted my enquiry entirely to those physical phenomena in which, owing to the circumstance of the case, unconscious muscular action, self deception, or even wilful fraud, would be rendered inoperative. I have not attempted to investigate except under such conditions of place, person, light, position, and observation, that contact was either physically impossible or could take place only under circumstances in which the unconscious or wilful movement of the hands could not vitiate the experiment. The experiments being tried in my own house, assumption of pre-arranged mechanical contrivances to assist the "medium" was out of the question.

The most curious thing regarding this article in the *Quarterly* is that the writer himself is a believer in a *new force*, and he arrogantly tries to put down any attempt to bring forward another. He refers to various hypotheses— to Sir William Hamilton's "latent thought," Dr. Laycock's "reflex action of the brain," and Carpenter's "ideo-motor principle." The reviewer adopts, without hesitation, Carpenter's hypothesis as the true and universal solvent of the phenomena in question, notwithstanding that this hypothesis is rejected by the physiologists most competent to judge it.

The whole tenor of the article, the numerous references to various "spiritual" phenomena, and the account of some of the reviewer's own experiences, show that he knows little or nothing of any such phenomena as those which I

D

have commenced to investigate. He refers to mesmerism, curative influence, "planchette" writing, table-tilting, table-turning, and to the messages obtained by these means. When he does not impute fraud, he explains the physical movements by the hypothesis of "unconscious muscular action," and the intelligence which sometimes controls these movements, delivers messages, etc., by "unconscious cerebration" or "ideo-motor action."

Now these explanations are possibly sufficient to account for much that has come under the personal cognisance of the reviewer. I will do him the justice to believe that, as he affirms, he did take every opportunity within his reach of witnessing the higher phenomena of "Spiritualism," and that on various occasions he met with results which were entirely unsatisfactory. The error into which he falls is this: Because he saw nothing that he thought worth following up, therefore it is impossible anyone else can be more fortunate. Because he and his scientific friends were following out the subject for more than a dozen years, therefore my own friends and myself deserve reprobation for pursuing the inquiry for about as many months.

According to this reasoning science would proceed very slowly. How often do we find instances of an abandoned investigation being taken up by another inquirer, who, more fortunate in his opportunities, carries it to a successful issue.

The reviewer has no grounds whatever for asserting that—

> "He (Mr. Crookes) altogether ignores the painstaking and carefully conducted researches which had led men of the highest scientific eminence to an unquestioning rejection of the whole of those higher phenomena of 'mesmerism' which are now presented under other names as the results of 'spiritual' or 'psychic' agency."

Now, I am quite familiar with these researches and with the various explanations of them so elaborately set forth by Dr. Carpenter and others. I made no reference to them, simply because the phenomena which came under their notice are entirely different from the phenomena I have examined. During my experiments I have seen plenty of instances of planchette writing, table-turning, table-tilting, and have received messages innumerable, but I have not attempted their investigation, mainly, for two reasons; first, because I shrank from the enormous difficulty and the consumption of time necessary to carry out an inquiry more physiological than physical; and, secondly, because little came under my notice in the way of messages or table-tilts which I could not account for.

My reviewer objects to the accordion being tried in a cage under the table. My object is easily explained. I must use my own methods of experiment. I deemed them good under the circumstances, and if the reviewer had seen the experiment before complaining it would have been more like a scientific man. But the cage is by no means essential, although, in a test experiment, it is an additional safeguard. On several subsequent occasions the accordion has played over the table, and in other parts of my room away from a table, the keys moving and the bellows action going on. An accordion was selected because it is absolutely impossible to play tricks with it when held in the manner indicated. I flatly deny that, held by the end away from the keys, the performance on an accordion "*with one hand* is a juggling trick often exhibited at country fairs," unless special mechanism exists for the purpose. Did ever the reviewer or anyone else witness this phenomenon at a country fair or elsewhere? The statement is only equalled in absurdity by the argument of a recent writer, who, in order to prove that the accounts of Mr. Home's levitations could not be true, says, "An Indian juggler could sit down in the middle of Trafalgar Square, and then slowly and steadily rise in the air to a height of five or six feet, still sitting, and as slowly come down again." Curious logic this, to argue that a certain phenomenon is impossible to Mr. Home because a country bumpkin or an Indian juggler can produce it.

In the experiment with the board and spring balance the reviewer says that "the whole experiment is vitiated by the absence of any determination of the *actual downward pressure* of Mr. Home's fingers."

I maintain that this determination is as unnecessary as a determination of his "downward pressure" on the chair on which he was sitting, or on his boots when standing. In reference to this point I said:—

"Mr. Home placed the tips of his fingers *lightly on the extreme end* of the mahogany board which was resting on the support."

"In order to see whether it was possible to produce much effect on the spring balance by pressure at the place where Mr. Home's fingers had been, I stepped upon the table and stood on one foot at the end of the board. Dr. Huggins, who was observing the index of the balance, said that the whole weight of my body (140 lbs.) so applied only sunk the index $1\frac{1}{2}$ lbs., or 2 lbs. when I jerked up and down. Mr. Home had been sitting in a low easy-chair, and could not, therefore, had he tried his utmost, have exerted any material influence on these results. I need scarcely add that his feet as well as his hands were closely guarded by all in the room."

"The wooden foot being $1\frac{1}{2}$ inches wide, and resting flat on the table, it is evident that *no amount of pressure* exerted within this space of $1\frac{1}{2}$ inches could produce any action on the balance."

But as this objection had been made by several persons, I devised certain experiments so as to entirely eliminate mechanical contact, and these experiments were fully described in my last paper.

To show the singular inaccuracy of the reviewer's statements and inferences, I give below, in parallel columns, quotations from the *Quarterly Review*, to mark the contrast between its unfair statements and my own actual language as printed in the *Quarterly Journal of Science*.

(*Quarterly Review*, Oct., 1871.)

"He admitted that he had not employed the tests which men of science had a right to demand before giving credence to the genuineness of those phenomena."

"He entered upon the inquiry, of which he now makes public the results, *with an avowed foregone conclusion of his own*."

"This obviously deprives his 'conviction of their objective reality' of even that small measure of value to which his scientific character might have given it a claim if his testimony had been impartial."

(*Quarterly Journal of Science July*, 1870.)

"My whole scientific education has been one long lesson in exactness of observation, and I wish it to be distinctly understood that this firm conviction [of the genuineness of certain phenomena] is the *result of most careful investigation*."

"In the present case I prefer to enter upon the inquiry with no preconceived notions whatever as to what can or cannot be." . . . "At first, I believed that the whole affair was a superstition, or at least an unexplained trick." . . . "I should feel it to be a great satisfaction if I could bring out light in any direction, and I may safely say that *I care not in what direction*." . . . "I cannot, at present, hazard even the most vague hypothesis as to the cause of the phenomena."

"*Views or opinions I cannot be said to possess* on a subject which I do not pretend to understand.". . . . . "The increased employment of scientific methods will promote exact observation and greater love of truth among enquirers, and will produce a race of observers who will drive the worthless residuum of Spiritualism hence into the unknown limbo of magic and necromancy."

On page 351 the reviewer insinuates that the early scientific training of myself and fellow-workers has been deficient. Speaking for myself, I may say that my scientific training could not have well commenced earlier than it did. Some time before I was sixteen I had been occupied in experimental work in a private physical laboratory. Then I entered the Royal College of Chemistry, under Dr. Hofmann, where I stayed six years. My first original research, on a complicated and difficult subject, was published when I was nineteen; and from that time to the present, my scientific education has been one continuous lesson in exactness of observation.

The following parallel passages show that my reviewer and myself differ but little in our estimates of the qualities required for scientific investigation :—

(Quarterly Review, Oct., 1871.)

"Part at least of this predisposition" [towards Spiritualism] "depends on *the deficiency of early scientific training.* Such training ought to include—1. The acquirement of habits of correct *observation* of the phenomena daily taking place around us; 2. The cultivation of the power of *reasoning* upon these phenomena, so as to arrive at *general principles* by the *inductive* process ; 3. The study of the method of testing the validity of such inductions by *experiment ;* and 4. The *deductive* application of principles thus acquired to the *prediction* of phenomena which can be verified by observation."

(Quarterly Journal of Science, July, 1870.)

"It will be of service if I here illustrate the modes of thought current among those who investigate science, and say what kind of experimental proof science has a right to demand before admitting a new department of knowledge into her ranks. We must not mix up the exact and the inexact. The supremacy of accuracy must be absolute." . . . "The first requisite is to be sure of *facts ;* then to ascertain *conditions ;* next, *laws.* Accuracy and knowledge of detail stand foremost amongst the great aims of modern scientific men. No observations are of much use to the student of science unless they are truthful and made under test conditions." . . . "In investigations which so completely baffle the ordinary observer, the thorough scientific man has a great advantage. He has followed science from the beginning through a long line of learning; and he knows, therefore, in what direction it is leading; he knows that there are dangers on one side, uncertainties on another, and almost absolute certainty on a third ; he sees to a certain extent in advance. But, where every step is towards the marvellous and unexpected, precautions and tests should be multiplied rather than diminished." . . . "Investigators must work ; although their work may be very small in quantity if only compensation be made by its intrinsic excellence."

The review is so full of perverse, prejudiced, or unwarranted mis-statements, that it is impossible to take note of them all. Passing over a number I had marked for animadversion, I must restrain myself to exemplifying a few of them.

The reviewer says that in my paper of July, 1870, my conclusion was "based on evidence which I admitted to be scientifically incomplete." Now in that paper I gave no experimental evidence whatever. After testifying emphatically as to the genuineness of two of the phenomena,

I gave an outline of certain tests which in my opinion ought to be applied, and, in a foot note, I said that my preliminary tests in this direction had been satisfactory. Is this admitting that I had not employed such tests? Is it fair to say that my results were "based on evidence which I admitted to be scientifically incomplete"?

On p. 346, referring to the results obtained with the board and balance, my reviewer urges that it never seems to have occurred to me "to test whether the same results could not be produced by throwing the board into rhythmical vibration by an *intentional* exertion of muscular action!" Yet will it be believed that at p. 344 he gives in my own words an account of my trying this identical experiment; and if he had taken the trouble to refer to my other paper on p. 486 of the *Quarterly Journal of Science*, he would have seen that I had tested in like manner the special apparatus to which he alludes. Has the reviewer learnt to blow both hot and cold? has his memory faded? or has chagrin at missing the truth in his long investigations spoilt his temper?

The "fact" spoken of on p. 347, that myself and friends attributed to psychic force the rippling of the surface of water in a basin, when it was really produced by the tremor of a passing railway train, is, like many other of the reviewer's "facts," utterly baseless; but as he is careful to tell us that in this particular case the "fact" is *not* one of his own invention, what is to be said of his discretion in believing his "highly intelligent witness"? No such occurrence took place; nor will a passing railway train produce a ripple on the surface of water in the basin in my room. I invite the "highly intelligent witness" to verify the fact.

On p. 348, in speaking of Mr. Varley, the reviewer says that his "scientific attainments are so cheaply estimated by those who are best qualified to judge of them, that he has never been admitted to the Royal Society." It seems natural it should follow that Mr. Varley *is* a Fellow of the Royal Society; he was elected in June last. I seem to be safe in saying exactly the opposite of the reviewer.

Not to weary the reader, I will deal only with three more mis-statements, selecting instances where the reviewer conceives that he is perfectly sure of his facts. In these three instances the reviewer commences his attack upon me with the ominous words "we speak advisedly." If this expression has any meaning, it implies that the writer is more than ordinarily certain of the statement it prefaces—that he speaks with deliberate and careful consideration. Now I also speak " advisedly" when I affirm, with the proof in my hand, that two if not all of these three charges fulminated against me are either heedless or wilful misrepresentations.

The first charge is as follows :—

> " Now we speak advisedly when we say that Mr. Crookes knew nothing whatever of the perseverance with which scientific men with whom he has never had the privilege of associating, qualified by long previous experience in inquiries of the like kind, had investigated these phenomena."

This spiteful statement is utterly false. I should think there are few persons in this country who have examined more carefully into the literature of the subject, or have read a greater number of books on Spiritualism, demonology, witchcraft, animal magnetism, spiritual theology, magic, and medical psychology, in English, French, and Latin. In this list I have even included Dr. Carpenter's article on Electro-Biology and Mesmerism in the *Quarterly Review* for October, 1853.

The second well-considered charge runs as follows :—

> " We also speak advisedly when we say that Mr. Crookes was entirely ignorant of the previous history of the subject, and had not even acquainted himself with the mode in which Professor Faraday had demonstrated the real nature of table-turning."

As to my entire ignorance of the previous history of the subject, that I think is pretty well disposed of in the preceding paragraph.

In 1853 I was intimately acquainted with the late Robert Murray, at that time manager at Mr. Newman's, Philosophical Iustrument Maker, Regent Street. I was in his shop several times a-week, and in May and June of that year, Murray and I had many conversations on the subject of table-turning. I well remember his telling me one day that Professor Faraday had given him the design of a test-apparatus by which he expected to prove that the rotation of the table was due to unconscious muscular action. A day or two after, he showed me the instrument which he was just about to send to Professor Faraday. At that time I was not unfrequently favoured by the late Rev. J. Barlow, Sec. R.I., with invitations to his house in Berkeley Street, and on one of these occasions on entering the room he thus accosted me:—"Mr. Crookes, I am glad you have come, we are doing a little table-turning, and have just been trying Faraday's new instrument. He is here, let me introduce you to him." Professor Faraday, in his kindly genial manner, explained to me fully the action of his instrument, and instead of pooh-poohing the remarks of a mere boy— for I was only 21—listened to my objection that his instrument was based upon the assumption that the supposed acting force from the hands would pass through the glass rollers, and replied that he had thought of that, and had got over the difficulty by tying the two boards together so as to render them rigid, when it was found that the table rotated as well with the instrument as without it.   Since then I have frequently employed this device of a long delicate indicator to magnify minute movements.   Perhaps my reviewer is not aware that this device is one of the commonest in physical laboratories, and was in frequent use long before any of the present generation saw the light. I have adopted it from 1853 up to the present time.   In my early experiments I availed myself of Professor Faraday's test-instrument, but recently when I have frequently made it a *sine qua non* that the operator shall not touch the table or any portion of the instrument, as in Experiments III., IV., VI., * it would puzzle even the ingenuity of my reviewer to say how Faraday's instrument is to be applied. In such cases I adopt the well-known and superlatively delicate index, a ray of light.

The *Quarterly* goes on to magnify Faraday's experiment on table-turning, utterly forgetting that Faraday did not come to a similar conclusion with the reviewer; at least, it was much more obscurely put if put at all.   Faraday, so far as I know, never spoke of a latent power within us, of which we are unconscious, working in our muscles, and leading them to acts which culminate in a form of speech or writing by movements of a table.   Faraday would have held this a sufficiently great novelty if put before him as I endeavour to put it before myself after reading the *Quarterly's* article.   My belief, however, is that Faraday experimented with questionable phenomena only.

The third charge in which the reviewer speaks "advisedly" runs thus:—

> "For this discovery [Thallium] he was rewarded by the Fellowship of the Royal Society ; but we speak advisedly when we say that this distinction was conferred on him with considerable hesitation."

In January, 1863, whilst the interest attaching to the discovery of the element Thallium was fresh in the minds of scientific men, I was both surprised and gratified at receiving the following note from Professor Williamson:—

---

* *Quarterly Journal of Science,* Oct., 1871, p. 487 *et seq.*

> " University of London,
>   Burlington House, W.,
>   16th Jan., 1863.
>
> "My dear Sir,—I should be glad to see your name on the list of Fellows of the Royal Society, and if you have no objection to my doing so, would do myself the honour of proposing you for election into the Society. Could you spare a quarter of an hour on Monday afternoon to talk the matter over with me at University College, and oblige
>
> "Yours very truly,
>
> "ALEX. W. WILLIAMSON."

This kindness being entirely unsought was the more pleasing to me. At the interview, my certificate was partially filled up and left in Professor Williamson's hands for the purpose of obtaining the necessary signatures. After this meeting with Professor Williamson I took no further steps in the matter, and spoke to no one on the subject; but in due time Professor Williamson wrote that my certificate was duly received at the Royal Society and read at the meeting, adding—

> "There is on the part of the Chemists now on the Council a sincere appreciation of your high claims."

Subsequently, the same kind friend wrote—

> "I have much pleasure in congratulating you and ourselves on your being one of the fifteen selected by the Council of the Royal Society for election."

I was formally elected on the 4th of June, 1863.

That discussion ensued when my name was brought before the Council follows as a matter of course. When fifteen only are to be elected from about fifty candidates, it is to be expected that the claims of each should be rigidly scrutinised; but whatever my anonymous reviewer may say "advisedly" on the subject, the *fact* remains that I was elected on the first application, an almost unheard-of honour for so young a man. Considering the large majority of eminent candidates whose election is postponed from year to year (sometimes even to ten years), there is no reason why my election should not have been postponed for at least one year, had there been truth in the statement that "considerable hesitation" was evinced in conferring this distinction upon me.

The grossness of the imputation, that the Royal Society admitted me although my investigations had only a merit purely *technical*, is astounding when the merits of the members generally are considered. I should consider them nearly all as purely technical workers in science, when they have done any work at all; but the curiosity is great when we find that the inquiry in question is purely technical.

Professedly, it is a question of apparatus.   In entering
upon an enquiry which I have endeavoured to keep within
the limits of broad, tangible, and easily demonstrable facts,
what qualities would common sense ask for in an investigator?   Would an investigation be considered trustworthy
were it conducted by a chemical dreamer who could spin
off theory by the hour, and cover acres of paper with chemical symbols, but who in a laboratory would be unable to
perform the simplest analysis, or build up a piece of chemical apparatus?   Let it not, however, be supposed that I am
unmindful of the philosophical and fructifying labours of
Hofmann, Williamson, and others, in the field of Chemical
Philosophy.   But with reference to this enquiry, surely it
should be conducted by one "who is trustworthy in an
enquiry requiring technical knowledge for its successful
conduct."

The reviewer assumes that the phenomenon of the sus-
pension of heavy bodies in the air, the up and down movements of a wooden board, and the registration of the
varying tension on a spring balance, are *psychical* not
physical; and he lays down a dictum that in such matter-
of-fact results which I have obtained, one's own eyes must
not be trusted, for in such a case "seeing is anything but
believing."   To show my unfitness for ascertaining the
weight of a piece of wood, he accuses me of being ignorant of the knowledge of Chemical Philosophy!   He does,
however, from his Olympian height, condescendingly admit
that my ability is *technical,* that I have made creditable
use of my very limited opportunities, and intimates that I
am trustworthy as to any enquiry which requires technical
knowledge for its successful conduct.   Now what does he
mean by all this?   I always thought that these qualities
which are so contemptuously accorded me were just those
of the highest value in this country.   What has chiefly
placed England in the industrial position she now holds
but technical science and special researches?

But my greatest crime seems to be that I am a "specialist
of specialists!"   I a specialist of specialists!   This is
indeed news to me, that I have confined my attention
only to one special subject.   Will my reviewer kindly
say what that subject is?   Is it general chemistry,
whose chronicler I have been since the commencement
of the "Chemical News" in 1859?   Is it Thallium,
about which the public have probably heard as much
as they care for?   Is it Chemical Analysis, in which
my recently published "Select Methods" is the result of

twelve years' work? Is it Disinfection and the Prevention
and Cure of Cattle Plague, my published report on which
may be said to have popularised Carbolic Acid? Is it
Photography, on the theory and practice of which my
papers have been very numerous? Is it the Metallurgy
of Gold and Silver, in which my discovery of the value of
Sodium in the amalgamation process is now largely used
in Australia, California, and South America? Is it in
Physical Optics, in which department I have space only to
refer to papers on some Phenomena of Polarised Light,
published before I was twenty-one; to my detailed description of the Spectroscope and labours with this instrument,
when it was almost unknown in England; to my papers on
the Solar and Terrestrial Spectra; to my examination of
the Optical Phenomena of Opals, and construction of the
Spectrum Microscope; to my papers on the Measurement
of the Luminous Intensity of Light; and my description
of my Polarisation Photometer? Or is my speciality
Astronomy and Meteorology, inasmuch as I was for twelve
months at the Radcliffe Observatory, Oxford, where, in
addition to my principal employment of arranging the
meteorological department, I divided my leisure time
between Homer and mathematics at Magdalen Hall,
planet-hunting and transit taking with Mr. Pogson,
now Principal of the Madras Observatory, and celestial
photography with the magnificent heliometer attached to
the Observatory? My photographs of the Moon, taken in
1855, at Mr. Hartnup's Observatory, Liverpool, were for
years the best extant, and I was honoured by a money
grant from the Royal Society to carry out further work in
connection with them. These facts, together with my trip
to Oran last year, as one of the Government Eclipse
Expedition, and the invitation recently received to visit
Ceylon for the same purpose, would almost seem to show
that Astronomy was my speciality. In truth, few scientific
men are less open to the charge of being "a specialist of
specialists."

Whilst the scepticism of this reviewer in respect to the
credibility of eminent witnesses, who give their names and
detailed statements of definite facts, exceeds all reasonable
bounds, his credulity in believing unattested statements of
others, or in expecting his readers to give credit to all the
absurd stories of his own experience, is refreshing in its
simplicity. He gives five separate accounts of certain
séances, where he saw something take place, but he con-
descends to few details; with one exception, no names or

tests are given, nor is there a single clue by which the accuracy of his statements can be verified. The only case in which a name and anything like detail is given is an account of a visit to Mr. Foster. Amongst other strange things here recorded, but by no means satisfactorily accounted for, even by our reviewer, is the following :—

> " We were not introduced to him by name, and we do not think that he could have had any opportunity of knowing our person. Nevertheless, he not only answered in a variety of modes the questions we put to him respecting the time and cause of the death of several of our departed friends and relatives whose names we had written down on slips of paper which had been folded up and crumpled into pellets before being placed in his hands ; but he brought out names and dates correctly in large red letters on his bare arm, the redness being produced by the turgescence of the minute vessels of the skin, and passing away after a few minutes like a blush."

The accurate answers to the reviewer's questions are supposed to be explained by "unconscious ideo-motor action," which, like "unconscious cerebration," is to explain all phenomena—past, present, and to come. Respecting the latter phenomenon he says—" The trick by which the red letters were produced was discovered by the enquiries of our medical friends." If the reviewer will not believe my plain statement of facts fortified by eminent witnesses, how does he expect his readers to believe these statements on the simple word of an anonymous writer ? His "gullibility," to use his own coarse, but expressive word, is strongly shown in his implicit belief of an obviously exaggerated account given by the well-known Robert Houdin of the way in which he and his son performed some of their tricks.

It is curious to note how Dr. Carpenter is made to pervade the *Quarterly Review* article. The reviewer throughout the article unconsciously manifests his implicit conviction that Dr. Carpenter is to be regarded as the paramount authority in reference to the subtle psychological questions involved in the so-called spiritualistic phenomena. The theories of the profound psychologists of Germany, to say nothing of those of our own countrymen, are made quite subsidiary to the hypotheses of Dr. William Carpenter. An unquestioning and infatuated belief in what Dr. Carpenter says concerning our mental operations has led the reviewer wholly to ignore the facts that these speculations are not accepted by the best minds devoted to psychological inquiries. I mean no disrespect to Dr. Carpenter, who, in certain departments, has done some excellent scientific work, not always perhaps in a simple and undogmatic spirit, when I "speak advisedly" that his mind lacks that acute, generalising, philosophic quality which would fit him to unravel the intricate problems which lie hid in the structure of the human brain.

Here I must bring this enforced vindication to a close. The self-reference to which I have been constrained is exceedingly distasteful to me. I forbear to characterise with fitting terms the spirit of this attack upon a scientific worker; it is enough that I have proved that in ten distinct instances the reviewer has deliberately calumniated me. It is a heavy and a true charge to bring against anyone occupying the reviewer's position amongst scientific men.

I cannot refrain from citing from the *Birmingham Morning News* the following trenchant criticism from the pen of an eminent chemist—himself a disbeliever in "Spiritualism." It will serve, as one instance amongst many, to show the feeling of disgust which the article in the *Quarterly Review* has excited among scientific men, whatever their opinions on this topic may be. After a few prefatory remarks, the writer goes on to say:—

"Either a new and most extraordinary natural force has been discovered, or some very eminent men specially trained in rigid physical investigation have been the victims of a most marvellous, unprecedented, and inexplicable physical delusion. I say unprecedented, because, although we have records of many popular delusions of similar kind and equal magnitude, and speculative delusions among the learned, I can cite no instance of skilful experimental experts being utterly, egregiously, and repeatedly deceived by the mechanical action of experimental test apparatus carefully constructed and used by themselves.

"As the interest in the subject is rapidly growing both wider and deeper, as a very warm discussion is pending, and further and still more extraordinary experimental revelations are in reserve, my readers will probably welcome a somewhat longer gossip on this than I usually devote to a single subject.

"Such an extension is the more demanded as the newspaper and magazine articles which have hitherto appeared, have, for the most part, by following the lead of the *Quarterly Review*, absurdly muddled the whole subject, and ridiculously mis-stated the position of Mr. Crookes and others. In the first place, all these writers that follow the *Quarterly* omit any mention or allusion to Mr. Crookes's preliminary paper published in July, 1870, but which has a most important bearing on the whole subject, as it expounds the object of all the subsequent researches.

"Mr. Crookes there states, that 'Some weeks ago the fact that I was engaged in investigating Spiritualism, so-called, was announced in a contemporary *(The Athenæum)*, and, in consequence of the many communications I have since received, I think it desirable to say a little concerning the investigations which I have commenced.   Views or opinions I cannot be said to possess on a subject which I do not protess to understand.   I consider it the duty of scientific men, who have learned exact modes of working, to examine phenomena which attract the attention of the public in order to confirm their genuineness, or to explain, if possible, the delusions of the honest, and to expose the tricks of deceivers.'   He then proceeds to state the case of Science *versus* Spiritualism, thus:—' The spiritualist tells of bodies weighing 50 or 100 lbs. being lifted up into the air without the intervention of any known force; but the scientific chemist is accustomed to use a balance which will render sensible a weight so small that it would take ten thousand of them to weigh one grain; he is, therefore, justified in asking that a power, professing to be guided by intelligence, which will toss a heavy body to the ceiling shall also cause his delicately-poised balance to move under test conditions.' ' The spiritualist tells of rooms and houses being shaken, even to injury, by superhuman power.   The man of science merely asks for a pendulum to be sent vibrating when it is in a glass case, and supported on solid masonry.'   'The spiritualist tells of heavy articles of furniture moving from one room to another without human agency.   But the man of science has made instruments which will divide an inch into a million parts, and he is justified in doubting the accuracy of the former observations, if the same force is powerless to move the index of his instrument one poor degree.'   ' The spiritualist tells of flowers with the fresh dew on them, of fruit, and living objects being carried through closed windows, and even solid brick walls.   The scientific investigator   naturally   asks   that   an   additional weight (if it be only the 1000th part of a grain) be deposited on one pan of his balance when the case is locked.   And the chemist asks for the 1000th part of a grain of arsenic to be carried through the sides of a glass tube in which pure water is hermetically sealed.'

"These   and   other   requirements   are   stated   by   Mr. Crookes, together with further exposition of the principles of strict inductive investigation, as it should be applied to such an inquiry.   A year after this he published an account of the experiments which I described in a former letter, and added to his own testimony that of the eminent physicist and astronomer Dr. Huggins, and Serjeant Cox. Subsequently, that is, in the last number of the *Quarterly Journal of Science*, he has published the particulars of another series of experiments.

" I will not now enter upon the details of these, but merely state that the conclusions of Mr. Crookes are directly opposed to those of the spiritualists. He utterly, positively, distinctly, and repeatedly repudiates all belief in the operations of the supposed spirits, or of any other supernatural agency whatever, and attributes the phenomena he witnessed to an entirely different origin, viz., to the direct agency of the medium. He supposes that the force analogous to that which the nerves convey from their ganglionic centres to the muscles, in producing muscular contraction, may, by an effort of the will, be transmitted to external inanimate matter, in such a manner as to influence in some degree its gravitating power, and produce vibratory motion. He calls this the *psychic force.*

"Now, this is direct and unequivocal *anti*-Spiritualism. It is a theory set up in opposition to the supernatural hypotheses of the spiritualists, and Mr. Crookes's position in reference to Spiritualism is precisely analogous to that of Faraday in reference to table-turning. For precisely the same reasons as those above quoted, the great master of experimental investigation examined the phenomena called table-turning, and he concluded that they were due to muscular force, just as Mr. Crookes concludes that the more complex phenomena he has examined are due to psychic force.

" Speaking of the theories of the spiritualists, Mr. Crookes, in his first paper (July, 1870), says:—

" 'The pseudo-scientific spiritualist professes to know everything. No calculations trouble his serenity; no hard experiments, no laborious readings; no weary attempts to make clear in words that which has rejoiced the heart and elevated the mind. He talks glibly of all sciences and arts, overwhelming the inquirer with terms like "electro-biologise," "psychologise," "animal magnetism," &c., a mere play upon words, showing ignorance rather than understanding.'

" And further on he says:—

" 'I confess that the reasoning of some spiritualists would almost seem to justify Faraday's severe statement—that many dogs have the power of coming to more logical conclusions.'

"I have already referred to the muddled mis-statement of Mr. Crookes's position by the newspaper writers, who almost unanimously describe him and Dr. Huggins as two distinguished scientific men who have recently been con-

verted to Spiritualism.   The above quotations, to which, if
space permitted, I might add a dozen others from either
the first, the second, or third of Mr. Crookes's papers, in
which he as positively and decidedly controverts the
dreams of the spiritualists, will show how egregiously these
writers have been deceived.   They have relied very naturally on the established respectability of the *Quarterly Review*,
and have thus deluded both themselves and their readers.
Considering the marvellous range of subjects these writers
have to treat, and the acres of paper they daily cover, it is
not surprising that they should have been thus misled in
reference to a subject carrying them considerably out of
their usual track; but the offence of the *Quarterly* is not so
venial.   It assumes, in fact, a very serious complexion when
further investigated.

" The title of the article is ' Spiritualism and its Recent
Converts,' and the ' recent converts ' most specially and
prominently named are Mr. Crookes and Dr. Huggins.
Serjeant Cox is also named, but not as a *recent* convert ;
for the reviewer describes him as an old and hopelessly
infatuated spiritualist.*   Knowing nothing of Serjeant
Cox, I am unable to say whether the reviewer's very
strong personal statements respecting him are true or
false—whether he really is ' one of the most gullible of
the gullible,' &c., though I must express my detestation
of the abominable bad taste which is displayed in the
attack which is made upon this gentleman.   The head
and front of his offending consists in having certified to the
accuracy of Mr. Crookes's account of certain experiments;
and for having simply done this, the reviewer proceeds, in
accordance with the lowest tactics of Old Bailey advocacy,
to bully the witness, and to publish disparaging personal
details of what he did twenty-five years ago.

" Dr. Huggins, who has had nothing further to do with
the subject than simply to state that he witnessed what Mr.

---

* It is due to Mr. Serjeant Cox to state that, so far from being an old
spiritualist, he had seen nothing of Spiritualism until he joined the Investigation Committee of the Dialectical Society, confident that he should thus assist
in dissipating a delusion or detecting an imposture; but by that elaborate
examination he was satisfied (as he states in his Report) that many of the
asserted phenomena are genuine, but that there was no evidence whatever to
support the theory of Spiritualism; that he was convinced by what he had seen
that the Force was a purely psychical one, and in no way produced by spirits of
the dead.   He is, in fact, a decided opponent of the theory of the spiritualists,
and has just published a book detailing his experiments, entitled "spiritualism
Answered by Science."   The writer of the article in the *Quarterly* must have
been quite aware of this fact, for he actually cites a passage from the letter to
me in which letter Mr. Serjeant Cox expressly repudiates the theory of Spiritualism.—W. C.

Crookes described, and who has not ventured upon one word of explanation of the phenomena, is treated with similar insolence.

" The reviewer goes out of his way to inform the public that Dr. Huggins is, after all, only a brewer, by artfully stating that 'like Mr. Whitbread, Mr. Lassell, and other brewers we could name, Dr. Huggins attached himself, in the first place, to the study of Astronomy.' He then proceeds to sneer at 'such scientific amateurs,' by informing the public that they 'labour, as a rule, under a grave disadvantage, in the want of that broad basis of scientific culture which alone can keep them from the narrowing and pervertive influence of a limited *specialism*.' The reviewer proceeds to say that he has 'no reason to believe that Dr. Huggins constitutes an exception' to this rule, and further asserts that he is justified in concluding that Dr. Huggins is ignorant of 'every other department of science than *the small subdivision of a branch* to which he has so meritoriously devoted himself.' Mark the words 'small subdivision of a branch.' Merely a twig of the tree of science is, according to this most unveracious writer, all that Dr. Huggins has ever studied.

"If a personal vindication were the business of this letter, I could easily show that these statements respecting the present avocations, the scientific training, and actual attainments of Dr. Huggins are most gross and atrocious misrepresentations; but Dr. Huggins has no need of my championship,—his high scientific position and the breadth and depth of his general attainments are sufficiently known to all in the scientific world, with the exception of the *Quarterly* reviewer. My object is not to discuss the personal question whether book-making and dredging afford better or worse training for experimental inquiry than the marvellously exact and exquisitely delicate manipulations of the modern observatory and laboratory, but to protest against this attempt to stop the progress of investigation, to damage the true interests of science and the cause of truth, by thus throwing low libellous mud upon any and every body who steps at all aside from the beaten paths of ordinary investigation. The true business of science is the discovery of truth, to seek it wherever it may be found, to follow the pursuit through bye-ways and high-ways, and, having found it, to proclaim it plainly and fearlessly, without regard to authority, fashion, or prejudice. If, however, such influential magazines as the *Quarterly Review* are to be converted into the vehicles of artful and elaborate efforts to

E

undermine the scientific reputation of any man who thus does his scientific duty, the time for plain speaking and vigorous protest has arrived. My readers will be glad to learn that this is the general feeling of the leading scientific men of the metropolis; whatever they may think of the particular investigations of Mr. Crookes, they are unanimous in expressing their denunciations of this article in the *Quarterly*.

"The attack upon Mr. Crookes is still more malignant than that upon Dr. Huggins. Speaking of Mr. Crookes's Fellowship of the Royal Society, the reviewer says, 'We speak advisedly when we say that this distinction *was conferred on him with considerable hesitation;*' and further, that 'We are assured, on the highest authority, that he is regarded among chemists as a specialist of specialists, *being totally destitute of any knowledge of chemical philosophy, and utterly untrustworthy as to any inquiry which requires more than technical knowledge for its successful conduct.*' The italics in these quotations are my own, placed there to mark certain statements to which no milder term than that of falsehood is applicable.

*   *   *   *   *   *

"If space permitted, I could go on quoting a long series of mis-statements of matters of fact from this singularly unveracious essay. The writer seems conscious of its general character, for, in the midst of one of his narratives, he breaks out into a foot-note, stating that '*This* is not an invention of our own, but a fact communicated to us by a highly intelligent witness, who was admitted to one of Mr. Crookes's *séances*.' I have taken the liberty to emphasise the proper word in this very explanatory note.

"The full measure of the injustice of prominently thrusting forward Dr. Huggins and Mr. Crookes as 'recent converts' to Spiritualism will be seen by comparing the reviewer's own definition of Spiritualism with Mr. Crookes's remarks above quoted. The reviewer says that 'The fundamental tenet of the spiritualist is the old doctrine of communication between the spirits of the departed and the souls of the living.' This is the definition of the reviewer, and his logical conclusion is that Mr. Crookes is a spiritualist because he explicitly denies the fundamental tenet of Spiritualism, and Dr. Huggins is a spiritualist because he says nothing whatever about it.

"If examining the phenomena upon which the spiritualist builds his 'fundamental tenet,' and explaining them in some other manner, constitutes conversion to Spiritualism, then the reviewer is a far more thorough-going convert than Mr. Crookes, who only attempts to explain the mild phenomena of his own experiments."

For six months past false and injurious reports concerning me and my recent investigations have been assiduously circulated in scientific circles. Although aware of their existence and their origin, I forbore to take public notice of them, thinking that their inherent falsehood would weight them too heavily to allow them to float long. The appearance of the *Quarterly* reviewer's attack on me, however, appears to have encouraged my culumniator, and, emboldened by my prolonged silence, a letter was sent to the *Echo* newspaper signed "B.,"* in which the writer put in a definite shape some of these ugly rumours, giving as his authority a certain "Mr. J." Not caring to carry on a paper war with an anonymous slanderer, I demanded that the mask should be dropped, when Mr. John Spiller, F.C.S., came briskly to the front, and in the *Echo* of November 6th accepted the responsibility of "B.'s" calumnies, adducing in corroboration of them a long letter he sent to me six months before—a letter having no relation whatever to the falsehoods related by "B."

A reply to definite accusations, made by a man possessing a certain reputation in the chemical world, is imperatively necessary, and regard for my own reputation makes me decide that my vindication shall be neither halting in language nor doubtful in meaning. And first let me show how little Mr. Spiller knows of the subject on which he speaks so positively. He came to my house unexpectedly one evening in April last, when Mr. Home and some friends had been dining with me. On that occasion nothing worth recording took place: in fact, it was not until some weeks later that my accordion was purchased, and my experimental apparatus devised. Mr. Spiller, however, appeared so struck with the little he did see that he begged me to invite him on similar occasions as often as I could. Mr. Serjeant Cox having given me a general permission to bring to his house any gentleman who took an interest in the subject, in accordance with this permission I invited Mr. Spiller to accompany me on April 25th to a strictly private party, when Mr. Home was expected. Had I thought him capable of committing so gross a breach of the laws of hospitality and good breeding as to publish a

---

* Echo, Oct. 31, 1871.

garbled and untruthful account of what took place in the privacy of a gentleman's dining-room, I should certainly have considered him not included in that general permission. However, we assembled, and before sitting down it was agreed by the gentlemen present that any objection on the score of suspected trick should be taken at the time, so that it might be subjected to instant proof or disproof. To this condition Mr. Spiller fully agreed.

The meeting at Mr. Serjeant Cox's was not one of my series of "test *séances*," as Mr. Spiller tries to make out, but was purely private, and quite unconnected with the experiments described in the *Quarterly Journal of Science.* It was a preliminary trial, to enable me to judge what class of phenomena could be easiest verified, and what sort of test apparatus I should devise. Mr. Spiller was never present at any test experiments, and saw Mr. Home only on the two occasions I have mentioned.

During the meeting at Mr. Serjeant Cox's many striking phenomena took place, and Mr. Spiller, being a stranger, was specially invited by Mr. Home to examine everything to his heart's content, and move about or get under the table whenever he liked. In accordance with my usual habit of taking notes, I was writing the whole time when I was not scrutinising the occurrences, and it was, therefore, easy not only to take down a description of the phenomena as they occurred, but also to record the actual words or comments used by each person present. From time to time I repeated aloud what I had written, and asked the company if it were correct; when any correction was supplied it was invariably adopted. The narrative of the proceedings was written in full immediately after, and a copy was sent to Mr. Spiller, as well as to others who had been present, for them to approve or alter. Mr. Spiller has dignified this paper by the name of an affidavit, whereas it was purely a private memorandum, never intended to be made public, and only drawn up so that each person might possess a thoroughly truthful account of what was considered at the time to be a very remarkable series of occurrences.

I have before me the paper which Mr. Spiller returned, corrected in pencil, and each correction signed with his initials. Where he has not corrected it is clear that he tacitly assents. His objections are of an utterly insignificant kind, and, comparing what he accepts with what he rejects, it will be seen that he strains at gnats while he swallows camels.

It now appears that Mr. Spiller totally disregarded the agreement assented to by all present—to speak out at the time, and thus to invite and facilitate the most searching inquiry. He arrogates to himself the position of an infallible judge instead of an honest inquirer. Whilst he professed to act openly and above-board, he was really carrying on furtive observations of his own. He recklessly discredits the other witnesses who were present, and expects the world to believe his own unsupported assertion. Brought forward at the time, his observations might have been of service, whilst at this distant date they are valueless. Mr. Spiller seems to imagine that, whilst everything else in nature is to be tested by careful experiment, his own hasty conclusions are to be accepted unchallenged.

The first accusation launched at me by Mr. Spiller is of a suppression of the truth. I am said to have recorded certain phenomena in the *Quarterly Journal of Science*, and to have ascribed their production to the action of a hitherto unknown form of force, notwithstanding that Mr. Spiller had explained to me six months previously the "tricks" by which these things were done.*

From the various forms under which this accusation has been repeated it appears that Mr. Spiller is trying to establish, either that he was present at the test experiments on which my papers in the *Quarterly Journal of Science* were based, or that these papers were but a narrative of what took place in his presence at Mr. Serjeant Cox's. Now I have published no narrative whatever, of any experiments at which Mr. Spiller was present, neither have I referred to them in any of my papers. His assertion, therefore, under whichever form it is viewed, is false.

In the *Echo* of November 10th I have gone fully into the analysis of these several accusations, and by placing in parallel columns extracts from Mr. Spiller's printed letters and statements, plainly convicted him in each case of a direct mis-statement of fact.

To show how ignorant I was of his reputed explanations of the few trifling things he thought he found out at Mr. Serjeant Cox's, and how unsuccessfully I begged him to give the information he now says I was aware of, I need only quote from a letter I wrote him on May 24th last. It runs as follows:—

"You have now for the third time given a very mysterious hint that you are in possession of a fact which would make me entirely alter my opinion about Mr. Home. Now I put it to you whether it would not be more consistent with

---

* *Echo*, Nov. 6, 1871.

our friendship for you to tell me fairly and candidly what you do know rather than keep me in suspense, week after week. You say it is impossible for you to write about it. That is a word I do not understand. If you will give me a plain statement of facts, and will not insinuate dishonest conduct on the part of myself and family, I promise you that I shall not only be very grateful to you, but will give what you tell me the most serious attention."

Mr. Spiller never came, and to my earnest appeal to put me in possession of his concealed facts I received no answer. And yet he has the audacity to say that I was perfectly aware of his explanation of the phenomena he witnessed!

But it is further reported that Mr. Spiller was my assistant during my test experiments, and found out at my house how the accordion "trick" was done.* Mr. Spiller was not my assistant, nor was he present at my house on any occasion when an accordion or any sort of apparatus was used. I refer to what he said about the only occasion when he ever saw an accordion in the same room with Mr. Home. I quote from a letter he wrote to me on May 3rd:†
—"The accordion business [at Mr. Serjeant Cox's] was rather curious, but then I was *not* under the table at the time of 'The Last Rose of Summer' being played." After experience of Mr. Spiller's logical method I am not surprised at the inference that this is the same thing as being under the table and finding out how the trick was done.

It would occupy too much space to re-state the accordion problem, but I will refer all who are interested to my description in the *Quarterly Journal of Science* for July last. If Mr. Spiller has really found out how this "trick" is done, why does he not publish it? for he would then have solved one of the most puzzling problems ever presented to his notice—a problem still unsolved by far wiser heads than his.

Debarred by the editor of the *Echo* from making further use of the columns of that journal, Mr. Spiller retreats to the pages of the *English Mechanic*,‡ where he reiterates accusations the falsity of which I have before exposed by means of his own letters. He complains that his previous perverse mis-statements and personal misrepresentations have brought him under sharp criticism. Of course they have; but this criticism is simply a consequence of his own unwarrantable attack. I cannot argue with my detractor about psychic force, or the explanation of the phenomena

---

recorded at my test *séances*, for the sufficing reason that he was never present at any of these experiments, and he has had no opportunity of knowing anything of the subject, except from my published papers. Professing to criticise my investigations, he carefully avoids all reference to any of these papers, and keeps harping on a weak remark of his own about the size of what he calls a "monster" locket attached to Mr. Home's watch-chain. A stranger to the circumstances would imagine that something very important turned upon the exact dimensions and reflecting power of this trinket. But what are the facts? In his letter to me of May 3rd,* speaking of an accordion which he saw playing at Mr. Serjeant Cox's in Mr. Home's hand, Mr. Spiller says that he "saw a flash of light whilst under the dining-room table"—a reflection from the "*shining surface*" of this locket; and on October 31st † his friend "B" gives (and he endorses) an entirely different tale about this light, which we are now told for the first time "was playing about Mr. Home's fingers as they lay in his lap,"—produced by the reflection from the "*polished reverse side*" of the locket in question. Speaking for myself, I saw nothing of this alleged light, nor did Mr. Home draw attention to it. My part in the transaction was simple. Mr. Spiller was the critical observer under the table on this occasion, and all I did was to write down what he said. In my notes written at the time, and acquiesced in by nine witnesses, I read—"Mr. Spiller declared that the accordion appeared self-luminous while it was playing." He subsequently denied this. He is welcome to do so, for it is a matter of no consequence whether he saw a light at all; the real question is, Did the accordion play and how was it played? Whether Mr. Spiller observed any light at all, the source of the light he said he saw, or the size of one of Mr. Home's trinkets, has nothing whatever to do with the subject of my investigations. The locket might be as big as a dinner-plate, and might be polished to the lustre of a speculum; the light it reflected might be as bright as the noon-day sun, and all that it would prove would be my calumniator's incompetency as an observer for not discovering it, or his inaccuracy as a witness for not mentioning it at the time when instant verification or disproof was possible.

Mr. Spiller speaks on one occasion of the "*shining surface*" of this locket; on another of its "*polished reverse*

---

* Echo, Nov. 6, 1871.   † Echo, Oct. 31, 1871.

side;" whilst on a third occasion he draws attention to the fact that platinum is "a white metal sometimes used for reflectors." Now to these inconsequential assertions I will oppose facts. The locket in question is now before me. Its obverse and reverse are almost identical, and the whole is so covered with ornamental engraving that there is not a particle of polished platinum about it. Moreover, on each side there are fifteen raised metallic ornaments of different shapes, which still further diminish the amount of light reflected from the surface. I have, moreover, carefully examined the optical properties of this locket. Tested in an accurate photometer, the reflecting power of each side is found to be equal to that of a silvered glass speculum 1·8 millimetres (less than 1-10th of an inch) square! I advise Mr. Spiller to keep silent about this "monster" locket in future, or, like a second Frankenstein, he will find he has conjured up a monster from his own inward consciousness which will devour his reputation.

But, of all the unfounded statements which my disingenuous assailant has circulated, the most outrageous is that he has been threatened with legal proceedings* because he refused to sign the narrative I sent him of the proceedings at his *séance* at Mr. Serjeant Cox's. Now, although the intrinsic absurdity of such a threat, made under the very eyes of a serjeant learned in the law, must be patent to everyone, it is necessary for me to state, which I do in the most emphatic manner, that this disgraceful accusation is *totally untrue*. I have never threatened Mr. Spiller with legal proceedings; I have never given him the remotest hint of such a thing; never did such a thought enter my mind ; and nothing that he has ever said or written in connection with this controversy could induce me for a moment to entertain the idea of legal proceedings.†

I hope I have now finished with the, to me, uncongenial task of combating perverse mis-statements and refuting personal misrepresentations ; and that I may be able to devote myself once more to quiet research.

---

* English Mechanic, Dec. 1, 1871.

† Since this was written Mr. Spiller has been made to withdraw his accusation (English Mechanic, Dec. 22, 1871). The ungracious manner in which he eats his offensive words " *I was threatened with legal proceedings* " shows that his anxiety to say something spiteful has led him to say the thing that was not.

CORRESPONDENCE

Upon DR. CARPENTER'S *asserted Refutation of* MR. W. CROOKES'S *Experimental Proof of the existence of a hitherto undetected Force.*

DR. W. B. CARPENTER, F.R.S., introduced into a Public Lecture an experiment which he alleged to be that upon which I had relied for proof of the existence of a hitherto undetected force. It was not my experiment, but an unjustifiable misrepresentation of it. Called upon to apologise for the wrong he had thus publicly done to me, Dr. Carpenter threw the responsibility from himself upon others whom he stated to have been his informants. I print the Correspondence, and leave it to the judgment of the scientific world.

WILLIAM CROOKES.

20, MORNINGTON ROAD, N.W.
February 21st, 1872.

PROFESSOR G. G. STOKES, SEC. R.S.

DEAR SIR,
My attention has been called to some statements publicly made by Dr. W. B. Carpenter, F.R.S., who gives you as the authority for some serious misrepresentations respecting myself.

On Friday, 19th January, 1872, Dr. Carpenter in a Lecture at the Vestry Hall, Chelsea, said:—

> "There was one fact of this kind in connection with Psychic Force which he would grapple with. Mr. William Crookes had sent a paper to the Royal Society last summer containing investigations into what he called a new force. It was returned to him by the Secretary, with a letter telling him that the Society would not refuse to receive papers upon the subject, but that some kind of scientific evidence ought to be given. Mr. Crookes afterwards sent in a second series of experiments. The Secretary did not like to refuse this paper on his own responsibility, so it came before the Council of the Royal Society; it was a most unusual thing for the Council to refuse a paper sent in by a member. Mr. Crookes's second paper came before the Council a month ago, and a Committee of two was appointed to examine it. They gave in their Report to the Council yesterday, and it was unanimously resolved that the paper be returned to him, as in the opinion of the Royal Society it was good for nothing. Anybody who had a pair of scales in the house could make an experiment to prove the fallacy of one of the points in Mr. Crookes's paper."

Dr. Carpenter here exhibited an experiment intended to show (and which some of his audience must have believed really did show) that I was ignorant of the merest rudiments of mechanics, and was deluded by an experiment the fallacy of which an intelligent schoolboy could have pointed out. He exhibited a glass of water poised against an equal weight upon a balance, and showed that by dipping a finger in water—that is, by *pressing* with a force exactly equal to the weight of the water displaced by the immersed finger—he increased the weight on that side of the balance. Now, unless the audience were intended to believe that I was ignorant of this childishly simple fact, and, further, that it completely accounted for the result of my experiment, for what purpose was this experiment shown?

A gentleman present who had read an account of my researches subsequently wrote to Dr. Carpenter, protesting against this misleading experiment being put forward as fairly representing what I had tried. In his reply to this protest, Dr. Carpenter says:—

> "So far from having been labouring to prejudice Mr. Crookes at the Royal Society, I did not even know of his having sent in a second paper until after it had been rejected by the Council. This rejection took place on Thursday afternoon, and I heard of it and the grounds of it from Professor Stokes and Sir Charles Wheatstone at the evening meeting. What I stated as to Mr. Crookes's experiment with the balance was *on their authority*,* as I shall be prepared to prove if the correctness of that statement is impugned."

Now, as a member of that Committee which decided on the rejection of my papers, you, of course, are aware that Dr. Carpenter's balance experiment wholly misrepresents my experiment. My illustrations showed you that the vessel of water was placed over the centre of the fulcrum. You had likewise read what I wrote in my last paper, that "immersing the hand to the utmost in the water, does not raise the level of the water sufficient to produce any movement whatever of the index of the balance."

From the construction of the instrument, as shown by the several drawings and photographs, and fully described in words, you would also have seen that not only was it impossible for any such effect to have taken place, but that the single experiment in which I employed water contact was one I had specially devised for the purpose of getting over some untenable objections raised by yourself against one of my early experiments.

My papers, as well as the illustrations accompanying them, therefore distinctly prove that I could not have made the blunder which Dr. Carpenter told a public audience I had committed ; and as Dr. Carpenter being pressed on the subject now endeavours to shift the burden of misrepresentation on to your shoulders, I shall feel obliged by your informing me if you really did make the statement which he attributes to you.

I remain,

Truly yours,

(Signed) WILLIAM CROOKES.

A similar letter was sent to Sir Charles Wheatstone. In due time I received the following replies :—

ATHENÆUM CLUB, PALL MALL.
February 28*th*, 1872.

DEAR SIR,

The conversation between Sir Charles Wheatstone, Dr. Carpenter, and myself, to which you allude in your letter of the 21st inst., has wholly passed out of my memory. It attracted no particular attention on my part, as I had no conception that a mere casual conversation in the tea-room of the Royal Society was going to be reproduced, with greater or less accuracy, at a public

---

* The italics are Dr. Carpenter's.

meeting. I can only speak with confidence of what I could or could not have said from the clear recollection I have of what I then knew.

You may recollect that in writing to you on the subject of your first paper, I stated as my own opinion, that the mere fact that a paper professed to establish the existence of a hitherto unrecognised force was no reason why a scientific Society should refuse to accept it, but *was* a reason why the experiments should be subjected to the most rigorous scrutiny. This position you accepted as perfectly fair and reasonable. I also pointed out conceivable modes of explaining the results of some of the experiments you described, by referring them to the action of perfectly well known causes. I did not maintain that the results were *actually produced* in the particular way I suggested, but only that they might reasonably be *conceived to have been so produced*, so that a person professing to establish the existence of a new force was bound to make his demonstration free from such objections.

Among other things, I pointed out that the glass vessel of water which you employed in one of your experiments rested on the board at some distance from the fulcrum; and that, consequently, when the hand was dipped into the water contained in the copper basin which, resting on a firm independent support, dipped into the water contained in the glass vessel, with which its interior was in communication by a hole, if time were given for the water to run through, the pressure on the base of the glass vessel would be increased by the weight of the water displaced by the hand, and consequently the spring balance would be affected.

Whether in the letter you wrote me in reply this particular point was noticed I do not at the moment recollect, nor does it signify, for in your second and third papers, one or both, I noticed particularly that you modified your experiment by placing the glass vessel with its middle over the fulcrum, and tested by direct experiment whether the insertion of the hand in the water in the copper vessel had any sensible effect on the balance.

These modifications I noticed particularly, as they had been made, as I presumed, expressly to meet certain objections which I had raised. It is quite impossible, therefore, that in my conversation with Dr. Carpenter, after your papers were ordered to be returned to you, I could have represented them to him as open to this objection. I *may* have talked to him on this subject (I don't know that I *did*), when your first paper alone had appeared; and, if so, it is conceivable that he may have confounded two conversations held, one several months ago, the other quite recently.

I wish to make one remark before I conclude. The question brought before the Committee of Papers of the Royal Society with reference to your papers was simply whether they should be accepted or declined. The decision of the Committee, as entered on the Minutes, was simply "declined." What estimate of the value of your papers each individual voter may have formed— what considerations mainly may have influenced him in giving his vote—are questions which he alone can answer; so that no one, as I conceive, has a right to add to the formal decision his notion of the grounds of it.

I am, Dear Sir,

Yours sincerely,

G. G. STOKES.

William Crookes, Esq., F.R.S.

---

19 Park Crescent, Portland Place, N.W.
March 14, 1872.

Dear Sir,

I did not state to Dr. Carpenter that the water experiment *disproved* the existence of your hypothetical psychic force; what I did say was to the effect that no argument in its favour could be deduced from the experiment which you put forward so prominently.

You say, page 20 of your first pamphlet, "I am now fitting up an apparatus in which contact is made through water in such way that transmission of mechanical movement to the board is impossible;" and again, at page 28, "As the mechanical transmission of power is by this means entirely cut off between the copper vessel and the board, the power of muscular control is thereby completely eliminated." In both these sentences you explain why you employed the interposition of water, and you state nothing from which I can infer that you had any other reason for doing so. It is further evident that in the experiments first communicated to Professor Stokes, the vessel of water was not placed directly over the fulcrum of the lever ; for you say (page 28), "In my first experiments with this apparatus, referred to in Professor Stokes's letter and my answer, the glass vessel was not over the fulcrum, but nearer B." That under such circumstances a mechanical pressure is exerted on the lever when the hand is dipped in the water is an undoubted fact ; whether it produces the effect in question or not depends on the sensibility of the apparatus and the placing of the vessel. A displacement of 3 cubic inches of water would exert a pressure which, if directly applied to your machine, would be equal to 6816 grains; the extreme pressure of your imaginary psychic force being, according to your own statement, 5000 grains. The fluctuation of the pressure in your experiment would naturally follow from the varying quantity of water displaced owing to the unsteadiness of the hand in the liquid.

From the above it appears to me that your experiment with the water vessel does not offer an iota of proof in favour of your doctrine of psychic force, or any disproof of the effect not being mechanical; though it might easily lead persons unacquainted with hydrostatic laws to infer that no mechanical pressure could be communicated under such circumstances.

I cannot see what part you intended the water to play when you subsequently placed the vessel over the dead point, and it appears to me contrary to all analogy that a force acting according to physical laws should produce the motion of a lever by acting on its fulcrum.

Yours faithfully,
C. WHEATSTONE.

W. CROOKES, Esq.

P.S.—I enclose a note which I have received from Dr. Carpenter.

UNIVERSITY OF LONDON,
BURLINGTON GARDENS, W.
Feb. 28, 1872.

DEAR SIR CHARLES,

If you should be communicating with Mr. Crookes on the subject as to which you spoke to me, it may be as well that you should let him know what was *my* understanding of the matter, as derived from yourself and Professor Stokes, and what was the account I gave of it in my Lecture.

I understood from you that Mr. Crookes had adduced the descent of a balanced vessel of water, on the immersion of Mr. Home's fingers into it, as a proof of the exertion of some force which could not be mechanical, and which must therefore be a *new* force, call it psychic, spiritual, or what you please. And I showed my audience that the immersion of the fingers into a tumbler of water so balanced would produce its descent simply by hydrostatic pressure; from which I drew the inference that Mr. Crookes's experiment gave no proof whatever of the existence of any force not known to us.

If I have in any way misunderstood your account of Mr. C.'s experiment, and have thereby done him injustice in my representation of it, I shall be quite ready to make any correction that you (as a mutual friend) may consider to be called for.

Believe me,
Yours faithfully,
WILLIAM B. CARPENTER.

SIR CHAS. WHEATSTONE.

20 MORNINGTON ROAD, N.W.

DEAR SIR CHARLES, *March 27th,* 1872.

You must allow me to protest against the experiments given in my Royal Society paper of September 27th, 1871, being ignored and the discussion being made to turn on a less decisive experiment referred to in an earlier paper. The experiments of September 27, 1871, are those referred to by Dr. Carpenter, and reported on by Professor Stokes and by yourself. That there is no doubt of this being the case is evident from Dr. Carpenter's language at Chelsea and elsewhere :—

" Mr. William Crookes had sent a paper to the Royal Society last summer [June 14th and June 28th, 1871] containing investigations into what he called a new force. It was returned to him by the Secretary. Mr. Crookes afterwards sent in a second series of experiments [September 27th, 1871]. The Secretary did not like to refuse this paper on his own responsibility, so it came before the Council of the Royal Society. . . . . Mr. Crookes's second paper came before the Council a month ago, and a Committee of two was appointed to examine it. They gave in their Report to the Council yesterday [January, 18th, 1872], and it was unanimously resolved that the paper be returned to him, as in the opinion of the Royal Society it was good for nothing.

" This rejection took place on Thursday afternoon [January 18th, 1872], and I heard of it and the grounds of it from Professor Stokes and Sir Charles Wheatstone at the evening meeting. What I stated as to Mr. Crookes's experiment with the balance was *on their authority.*"

Dr. Carpenter here explicitly refers to the experiments given in my paper of September 27th, 1871, and not only says that you mentioned to him the grounds of the rejection of that paper on the very day it occurred, but that you described to him one of the experiments given in it.

I must therefore object to having the discussion drawn from the point at issue, from the testing experiment in question presented to the Royal Society, to an imperfect form of the same experiment which was merely referred to in a paper published elsewhere.

From my pamphlet reprinted from the " Quarterly Journal of Science" for October 1st, 1871 (page 28), you quote the following words :—

" As the mechanical transmission of power is by this means entirely cut off between the copper vessel and the board, the power of muscular control is thereby completely eliminated."

You also quote a foot-note in which I refer to an early and imperfect form of the experiment, and you thereupon comment on these passages, speak of well-known hydrostatic laws, and give calculations, as if my published experiments in question really afforded any grounds for severe remarks.

It is much to be regretted that you should have selected from my pamphlet two passages occurring on page 28, and should have omitted to read the few lines which connect these passages; otherwise it must have been apparent to you that your self-evident exposition of a well-known hydrostatic law had no bearing on the case in point.

Let me supply the deficiency. The following paragraph, from page 28 of my pamphlet, fills up the gap between the two passages you quote :—

" *On the board, exactly over the fulcrum,* is placed a large glass vessel filled with water, I. L is a massive iron stand furnished with an arm and a ring, M N, in which rests a hemispherical copper vessel, perforated with several holes in the bottom. The iron stand is 2 inches from the board, A B, and the arm and copper vessel, M N, are so adjusted that the latter dips into the water 1½ inches, being 5½ inches from the bottom of I, and 2 inches from its circumference. Shaking or striking the arm M or the vessel N produces no appreciable mechanical effect on the board A B capable of affecting the balance. *Dipping the hand to the fullest extent into the water in* N *does not produce the least appreciable action on the balance.* As the mechanical transmission of power is by this means entirely cut off between the copper vessel and the board A B, the power of muscular control is thereby eliminated."

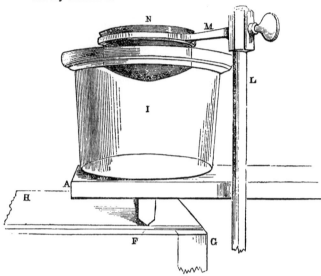

I venture to think that had you read the above connecting link between your two quotations from my pamphlet, or had even noticed the parts I have italicised, you would not have written,—

" That under such circumstances a mechanical pressure is exerted on the lever when the hand is dipped in the water is an undoubted fact ; whether it produces the effect in question or not depends on the sensibility of the apparatus and the placing of the vessel. A displacement of 3 cubic inches of water would exert a pressure which, if directly applied to your machine, would be equal to 6816 grains ; the extreme pressure of your imaginary psychic force being, according to your own statement, 5000 grains."

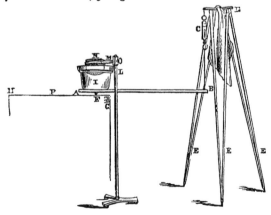

I have preferred to quote from the reprint of my paper in the "Quarterly Journal of Science" for October 1st, 1871, as your citations appear to show that you have derived your information from it; but in my Royal Society communication of September 27th, 1871—the paper to which Dr. Carpenter and yourself referred—the same experiment is described in almost identical words, and is, moreover, illustrated with photographs of the apparatus.

But why refer only to the water-contact experiment? The true explanation is the one which will reconcile all the indisputable facts. How does the well-known hydrostatic law account for Experiment 2 on p. 29, in which the vessel of water was removed? Or Experiment 3, in which the force acted through a space of 1 foot? Or Experiment 4, in which the force acted at a distance of 3 feet? Or Experiments 5 and 6, in which another kind of apparatus was used, and the force likewise acted at a distance?

The only sentence in your letter bearing in any way on my actual experiment is the last one, in which you say:—

> "I cannot see what part you intended the water to play when you subsequently placed the vessel over the dead point, and it appears to me contrary to all analogy that a force acting according to physical laws should produce the motion of a lever by acting on its fulcrum."

In this I entirely agree. I too cannot see the part the water played; nor can I trace the analogy between the psychic force and a force acting according to known physical laws. Yet the facts recorded in my papers are true for all that.

I remain,

Truly yours,

WILLIAM CROOKES.

Sir Charles Wheatstone, F.R.S., &c.

TO THE PRESIDENT AND COUNCIL OF THE ROYAL SOCIETY.

20 Mornington Road, N.W.,

March 30th, 1872.

Gentlemen,

I beg to bring to your notice the fact that on two recent occasions the secret proceedings of your Council have been made public, contrary to the honourable and salutary practice which has hitherto prevailed.

In an article in the "Quarterly Review" (No. 262, p. 343), understood to be written by Dr. W. B. Carpenter, F.R.S., the reviewer says:—

> "For this discovery he [*i.e.*, myself] was rewarded by the Fellowship of the Royal Society; but we speak advisedly when we say that this distinction was conferred on him with considerable hesitation, the ability he displayed in the investigation being purely technical."

No one, it is clear, has a right to reveal what takes place in the private deliberations of the Council. In the discussions about the eligibility of the various candidates for the Fellowship, there must necessarily be a comparison of claims, a full consideration of the merits of each individual; not only must a man's intellectual powers be canvassed, but his moral and social character must be discussed. If, however, these discussions are afterwards to be revealed and *published*, no man's character, after his name has been put in nomination for the Royal Society, will be safe from charges founded on hearsay and imperfect evidence.

Again, on Friday, January 19th, 1872, Dr. Carpenter, in a Lecture at the Vestry Hall, Chelsea, speaking of a paper which has recently come before you, stated that—

> "Mr. Crookes's second paper came before the Council [of the Royal Society] a month ago, and a committee of two was appointed to examine

it. They gave in their report yesterday [Jan. 18th, 1872], and it was unanimously resolved that the paper be returned to him, as, in the opinion of the Royal Society, it was good for nothing."

Dr. Carpenter is not a member of your Council; what he states must, therefore, if true, be the result of hearsay; and when the rejected paper was returned to me on January 18th, it was unaccompanied by any remarks tending to confirm the opinion attributed by Dr. Carpenter to the Royal Society.

I repeat, that if the private deliberations of the Council of the Royal Society are to be made public in this informal and irresponsible manner, the character and scientific *status* of every member of the Society will be at the mercy of any lecturer who may proclaim that he is in the secret of your deliberations.

That the worth of each paper treating of new and exciting topics should be the subject of minute and even personal discussion is from the nature of the case inevitable; but if portions of those discussions separated from the accompanying and modifying circumstances are to be published on no better authority than the perverted statement of one who pretends he has had reported to him the substance of the controversy, members of the Council will either withhold the free expression of their opinions, or their deliberations will go forth to the world distorted with the prejudices of invidious talkers.

Therefore, I respectfully beg the Council of the Royal Society will so deal with this matter as to deter, for the future, any Fellow from betraying and publishing deliberations which ought to be held inviolate.

I am, Gentlemen,

Your obedient Servant,

WILLIAM CROOKES.

———

THE ROYAL SOCIETY,

BURLINGTON HOUSE, LONDON, W.

18th April, 1872.

DEAR SIR,

Your letter of March 30th to the President and Council of the Royal Society, was laid before them at their meeting held to-day. They passed the following Resolutions:—

Resolved—(1.)   That the President and Council regret that statements in question should have been published, both because they are incorrect in point of fact, and because the unauthorised publication of the deliberations of the Council is contrary to the usage of the Society.

(2.)   That the above Resolution be communicated to Mr. Crookes.

I am, Dear Sir,

Yours faithfully,

G. G. STOKES, Sec. R.S

Wm. Crookes, Esq., F.R.S.

RESEARCHES

IN THE

PHENOMENA OF SPIRITUALISM.

By WILLIAM CROOKES, F.R.S., &c.

PART III.

NOTES OF AN INQUIRY INTO THE
PHENOMENA CALLED SPIRITUAL,
DURING THE YEARS 1870-73.

TO WHICH ARE ADDED

THREE LETTERS, ENTITLED " MISS FLORENCE COOK'S MEDIUM-
SHIP," " SPIRIT-FORMS," AND " THE LAST OF KATIE KING;
THE PHOTOGRAPHING OF KATIE KING BY THE AID OF THE
ELECTRIC LIGHT."

PRICE ONE SHILLING.

LONDON:

J. BURNS, 15 SOUTHAMPTON ROW, W.C.

H. NISBET, PRINTER, 219 GEORGE STREET, GLASGOW.

REPRINTED FROM THE QUARTERLY JOURNAL OF SCIENCE.

RESEARCHES

IN THE

PHENOMENA OF SPIRITUALISM.

By WILLIAM CROOKES, F.R.S., &c.

In One Volume, Handsome Cloth, price 5s.

This Work is also Published in Three Parts, price One Shilling each.

PART I.

SPIRITUALISM

VIEWED BY THE LIGHT OF MODERN SCIENCE,

AND

EXPERIMENTAL INVESTIGATIONS ON PSYCHIC FORCE,

With 16 Illustrations and Diagrams. Price 1s.

PART II.

PSYCHIC FORCE AND MODERN SPIRITUALISM,

A REPLY TO THE *Quarterly Review* AND OTHER CRITICS,

To which is added Correspondence upon Dr. Carpenter's Asserted Refutation of the Author's Experimental Proof of the Existence of a hitherto Undetected Force.

With Two Illustrations. Price 1s.

PART III.

NOTES OF AN INQUIRY

INTO THE

PHENOMENA CALLED SPIRITUAL,

DURING THE YEARS 1870-73.

To which are added Three Letters, entitled "Miss Florence Cook's Mediumship," "Spirit-Forms," and "The Last of Katie King; the Photographing of Katie King by the aid of the Electric Light."

Price 1s.

LONDON:

J. BURNS, 15 SOUTHAMPTON ROW, HOLBORN, W.C.

NOTES OF AN ENQUIRY INTO THE PHENOMENA CALLED SPIRITUAL,

DURING THE YEARS 1870-73.*

L IKE a traveller exploring some distant country, the wonders of which have hitherto been known only through reports and rumours of a vague or distorted character, so for four years have I been occupied in pushing an enquiry into a territory of natural knowledge which offers almost virgin soil to a scientific man. As the traveller sees in the natural phenomena he may witness the action of forces governed by natural laws, where others see only the capricious intervention of offended gods, so have I endeavoured to trace the operation of natural laws and forces, where others have seen only the agency of supernatural beings, owning no laws, and obeying no force but their own free will. As the traveller in his wanderings is entirely dependent on the goodwill and friendliness of the chiefs and the medicine men of the tribes amongst whom he sojourns, so have I not only been aided in my enquiry in a marked degree by some of those who possess the peculiar powers I have sought to examime, but have also formed firm and valued friendships amongst many of the recognised leaders of opinion, whose hospitalities I have shared. As the traveller sometimes sends home, when opportunity offers, a brief record of progress, which record, being necessarily isolated from all that has led up to it, is often received with disbelief or ridicule, so have I on two occasions selected and published what seemed to be a few striking and definite *facts;* but having omitted to describe the preliminary stages necessary to lead the public mind up to an appreciation of the phenomena and to show how they fitted into other observed facts, they were also met, not only with incredulity, but with no little abuse. And, lastly, as the traveller, when his exploration is finished and he returns to his old associates, collects together all his scattered notes, tabulates them, and puts them in order ready to be given to the world as a connected narrative, so have I, on reaching this stage of the enquiry, arranged and put together all my disconnected observations ready to place before the public in the form of a volume.

* First published in the *Quarterly Journal of Science* for January, 1874.

The phenomena I am prepared to attest are so extraordinary and so directly oppose the most firmly rooted articles of scientific belief—amongst others, the ubiquity and invariable action of the force of gravitation—that, even now, on recalling the details of what I witnessed, there is an antagonism in my mind between *reason*, which pronouces it to be scientifically impossible, and the consciousness that my senses, both of touch and sight,—and these corroborated, as they were, by the senses of all who were present,—are not lying witnesses when they testify against my preconceptions.*

But the supposition that there is a sort of mania or delusion which suddenly attacks a whole roomful of intelligent persons who are quite sane elsewhere, and that they all concur to the minutest particulars, in the details of the occurrences of which they suppose themselves to be witnesses, seems to my mind more incredible than even the facts they attest.

The subject is far more difficult and extensive than it appears. Four years ago I intended only to devote a leisure month or two to ascertain whether certain marvellous occurrences I had heard about would stand the test of close scrutiny. Having, however, soon arrived at the same conclusion as, I may say, every impartial enquirer, that there was "something in it," I could not, as a student of nature's laws, refuse to follow the enquiry wheresoever the facts might lead. Thus a few months have grown into a few years, and were my time at my own disposal it would probably extend still longer. But other matters of scientific and practical interest demand my present attention ; and, inasmuch as I cannot afford the time requisite to follow the enquiry as it deserves, and as I am fully confident it will be studied by scientific men a few years hence, and as my

---

* The following remarks are so appropriate that I cannot forbear quoting them. They occur in a private letter from an old friend, to whom I had sent an account of some of these occurrences. The high position which he holds in the scientific world renders doubly valuable any opinion he expresses on the mental tendencies of scientific men. "Any *intellectual* reply to your facts I cannot see. Yet it is a curious fact that even I, with all my tendency and desire to believe spiritualistically, and with all my faith in your power of observing and your thorough truthfulness, feel as if I wanted to see for myself ; and it is quite painful to me to think how much more proof I want. Painful, I say, because I see that it is not reason which convinces a man, unless a fact is repeated so frequently that the impression becomes like a habit of mind, an old acquaintance, a thing known so long that it cannot be doubted. This is a curious phase of man's mind, and it is remarkably strong in scientific men—stronger than in others, I think. For this reason we must not always call a man dishonest because he does not yield to evidence for a long time. The old wall of belief must be broken by much battering."

opportunities are not now as good as they were some time ago, when Mr. D. D. Home was in good health, and Miss Kate Fox (now Mrs. Jencken) was free from domestic and maternal occupations, I feel compelled to suspend further investigation for the present.

To obtain free access to some persons abundantly endowed with the power I am experimenting upon, now involves more favour than a scientific investigator should be expected to make of it. Spiritualism amongst its more devout followers is a religion. The mediums, in many cases young members of the family, are guarded with a seclusion and jealousy which an outsider can penetrate with difficulty. Being earnest and conscientious believers in the truth of certain doctrines which they hold to be substantiated by what appear to them to be miraculous occurrences, they seem to hold the presence of scientific investigation as a profanation of the shrine. As a personal favour I have more than once been allowed to be present at meetings that presented rather the form of a religious ceremony than of a spiritualistic *séance*. But to be admitted by favour once or twice, as a stranger might be allowed to witness the Eleusinian mysteries, or a Gentile to peep within the Holy of Holies, is not the way to ascertain facts and discover laws. To gratify curiosity is one thing; to carry on systematic research is another. I am seeking the truth continually. On a few occasions, indeed, I have been allowed to apply tests and impose conditions; but only once or twice have I been permitted to carry off the priestess from her shrine, and in my own house, surrounded by my own friends, to enjoy opportunities of testing the phenomena I had witnessed elsewhere under less conclusive conditions.* My observations on these cases will find their due place in the work I am about to publish.

Following the plan adopted on previous occasions,—a plan which, however much it offended the prejudices of some critics, I have good reason to know was acceptable to the readers of the "Quarterly Journal of Science,"—I intended to embody the results of my labour in the form of one or two articles for this journal. However, on going over my notes, I find such a wealth of facts, such a superabundance of evidence, so overwhelming a mass of testi-

---

* In this paper I give no instances and use no arguments drawn from these exceptional cases. Without this explanation it might be thought that the immense number of facts I have accumulated were principally obtained on the few occasions here referred to, and the objection would naturally arise of insufficiency of scrutiny from want of time.

mony, all of which will have to be marshalled in order, that I could fill several numbers of the " Quarterly." I must therefore be content on this occasion with an outline only of my labours, leaving proofs and full details to another occasion.

My principal object will be to place on record a series of actual occurrences which have taken place in my own house, in the presence of trustworthy witnesses, and under as strict test conditions as I could devise. Every fact which I have observed is, moreover, corroborated by the records of independent observers at other times and places. It will be seen that the facts are of the most astounding character, and seem utterly irreconcilable with all known theories of modern science. Having satisfied myself of their *truth*, it would be moral cowardice to withhold my testimony because my previous publications were ridiculed by critics and others who knew nothing whatever of the subject, and who were too prejudiced to see and judge for themselves whether or not there was truth in the phenomena ; I shall state simply what I have seen and proved by repeated experiment and test, and " I have yet to learn that it is irrational to endeavour to discover the causes of unexplained phenomena."

At the commencement, I must correct one or two errors which have taken firm possession of the public mind. One is that *darkness* is essential to the phenomena. This is by no means the case. Except where darkness has been a necessary condition, as with some of the phenomena of luminous appearances, and in a few other instances, everything recorded has taken place *in the light*. In the few cases where the phenomena noted have occurred in darkness I have been very particular to mention the fact ; moreover some special reason can be shown for the exclusion of light, or the results have been produced under such perfect test conditions that the suppression of one of the senses has not really weakened the evidence.

Another common error is that the occurrences can be witnessed only at certain times and places,—in the rooms of the medium, or at hours previously arranged ; and arguing from this erroneous supposition, an analogy has been insisted on between the phenomena called spiritual and the feats of legerdemain by professional " conjurers " and " wizards," exhibited on their own platform and surrounded by all the appliances of their art.

To show how far this is from the truth, I need only say that, with very few exceptions, the many hundreds of facts

I am prepared to attest,—facts which to imitate by known mechanical or physical means would baffle the skill of a Houdin, a Bosco, or an Anderson, backed with all the resources of elaborate machinery and the practice of years,—have all taken place in my own house, at times appointed by myself, and under circumstances which absolutely precluded the employment of the very simplest instrumental aids.

A third error is that the medium must select his own circle of friends and associates at a *seance;* that these friends must be thorough believers in the truth of whatever doctrine the medium enunciates; and that *conditions* are imposed on any person present of an investigating turn of mind, which entirely preclude accurate observation and facilitate trickery and deception. In reply to this I can state that, (with the exception of the very few cases to which I have alluded in a previous paragraph * where, whatever might have been the motive for exclusiveness, it certainly was not the veiling of deception), I have chosen my own circle of friends, have introduced any hard-headed unbeliever whom I pleased, and have generally imposed my own terms, which have been carefully chosen to prevent the possibility of fraud. Having gradually ascertained some of the conditions which facilitate the occurrence of the phenomena, my modes of conducting these inquiries have generally been attended with equal and, indeed, in most cases with more, success than on other occasions, where, through mistaken notions of the importance of certain trifling observances, the conditions imposed might render less easy the detection of fraud.

I have said that darkness is not essential. It is, however, a well-ascertained fact that when the force is weak a bright light exerts an interfering action on some of the phenomena. The power possessed by Mr. Home is sufficiently strong to withstand this antagonistic influence; consequently, he always objects to darkness at his *séances.* Indeed, except on two occasions, when, for some particular experiments of my own, light was excluded, everything which I have witnessed with him has taken place in the light. I have had many opportunities of testing the action of light of different sources and colours, such as sun-light, diffused day light, moon light, gas, lamp, and candle light, electric light from a vacuum tube, homogeneous yellow light, &c. The interfering rays appear to be those at the extreme end of the spectrum.

---

* See note on page 83.

I now proceed to classify some of the phenomena which have come under my notice, proceeding from the simple to the more complex, and briefly giving under each heading an outline of some of the evidence I am prepared to bring forward. My readers will remember that, with the exception of cases specially mentioned, the occurrences have taken place *in my own house, in the light, and with only private friends present* besides the medium. In the contemplated volume I propose to give in full detail the tests and precautions adopted on each occasion, with names of witnesses. I only briefly allude to them in this article.

CLASS I.

The Movement of Heavy Bodies with Contact, but without Mechanical Exertion.

This is one of the simplest forms of the phenomena observed. It varies in degree from a quivering or vibration of the room and its contents to the actual rising into the air of a heavy body when the hand is placed on it. The retort is obvious that if people are touching a thing when it moves, they push it, or pull it, or lift it; I have proved experimentally that this is. not the case in numerous instances, but as a matter of evidence I attach little importance to this class of phenomena by itself, and only mention them as a preliminary to other movements of the same kind, but without contact.

These movements and indeed I may say the same of every kind of phenomenon are generally preceded by a peculiar cold air, sometimes amounting to a decided wind. I have had sheets of paper blown about by it, and a thermometer lowered several degrees. On some occasions, which I will subsequently give more in detail, I have not detected any actual movement of the air, but the cold has been so intense that I could only compare it to that felt when the hand has been within a few inches of frozen mercury.

CLASS II.

The Phenomena of Percussive and other Allied Sounds.

The popular name of "raps" conveys a very erroneous impression of this class of phenomena. At different times, during my experiments, I have heard delicate ticks, as with the point of a pin ; a cascade of sharp sounds as from an induction coil in full work ; detonations in the air ; sharp metallic taps ; a cracking like that heard when a frictional machine is at work; sounds like scratching; the twittering as of a bird, &c.

These sounds are noticed with almost every medium, each having a special peculiarity; they are more varied with Mr. Home, but for power and certainty I have met with no one who at all approached Miss Kate Fox. For several months I enjoyed almost unlimited opportunity of testing the various phenomena occurring in the presence of this lady, and I especially examined the phenomena of these sounds. With mediums, generally, it is necessary to sit for a formal *séance* before anything is heard; but in the case of Miss Fox it seems only necessary for her to place her hand on any substance for loud thuds to be heard in it, like a triple pulsation, sometimes loud enough to be heard several rooms off. In this manner I have heard them in a living tree—on a sheet of glass—on a stretched iron wire—on a stretched membrane—a tambourine—on the roof of a cab—and on the floor of a theatre. Moreover, actual contact is not always necessary; I have had these sounds proceeding from the floor, walls, &c., when the medium's hands and feet were held—when she was standing on a chair—when she was suspended in a swing from the ceiling—when she was enclosed in a wire cage—and when she had fallen fainting on a sofa. I have heard them on a glass harmonicon—I have felt them on my own shoulder and under my own hands. I have heard them on a sheet of paper, held between the fingers by a piece of thread passed through one corner. With a full knowledge of the numerous theories which have been started, chiefly in America, to explain these sounds, I have tested them in every way that I could devise, until there has been no escape from the conviction that they were true objective occurrences not produced by trickery or mechanical means.

An important question here forces itself upon the attention. *Are the movements and sounds governed by intelligence?* At a very early stage of the inquiry, it was seen that the power producing the phenomena was not merely a blind force, but was associated with or governed by intelligence: thus the sounds to which I have just alluded will be repeated a definite number of times, they will come loud or faint, and in different places at request; and by a pre-arranged code of signals, questions are answered, and messages given with more or less accuracy.

The intelligence governing the phenomena is sometimes manifestly below that of the medium. It is frequently in direct opposition to the wishes of the medium: when a determination has been expressed to do something which might not be considered quite right, I have known urgent messages given to induce a reconsideration. The intelligence is sometimes of such a character as to lead to the belief that it does not emanate from any person present.

Several instances can be given to prove each of these statements, but the subject will be more fully discussed subsequently, when treating of the source of the intelligence.

CLASS III.

The Alteration of Weight of Bodies.

I have repeated the experiments already described in this Journal, in different forms, and with several mediums. I need not further allude to them here.

CLASS IV.

Movements of Heavy Substances when at a Distance from the Medium.

The instances in which heavy bodies, such as tables, chairs, sofas, &c. have been moved, when the medium has not been touching them, are very numerous. I will briefly mention a few of the most striking. My own chair has been twisted partly round, whilst my feet were off the floor. A chair was seen by all present to move slowly up to the table from a far corner, when all were watching it ; on another occasion an arm chair moved to where we were sitting, and then moved slowly back again (a distance of about three feet) at my request. On three successive evenings a small table moved slowly across the room, under conditions which I had specially pre-arranged, so as to answer any objection which might be raised to the evidence. I have had several repetitions of the experiment considered by the Committee of the Dialectical Society to be conclusive, viz., the movement of a heavy table in full light, the chairs turned with their backs to the table, about a foot off, and each person kneeling on his chair, with hands resting over the backs of the chair, but not touching the table. On one occasion this took place when I was moving about so as to see how every one was placed.

CLASS V.

The Rising of Tables and Chairs off the ground, without contact with any person.

A remark is generally made when occurrences of this kind are mentioned, Why is it only tables and chairs which do these things? Why is this property peculiar to furniture? I might reply that I only observe and record facts, and do not profess to enter into the Why and Wherefore; but indeed it will be obvious that if a heavy inanimate body in an ordinary dining-room has to rise off the floor, it cannot very well be anything else but a table or a chair. That this propensity is not specially attached to furniture, I have abundant evidence; but, like other experimental demonstrators, the intelligence or power, whatever it may be, which produces these phenomena can only work with the materials which are available.

On five separate occasions, a heavy dining-table rose between a few inches and $1\frac{1}{2}$ feet off the floor, under special circumstances, which rendered trickery impossible. On another occasion, a heavy table rose from the floor in full light, while I was holding the medium's hands and feet. On another occasion the table rose from the floor, not only when no person was touching it, but under conditions which I had pre-arranged so as to assure unquestionable proof of the fact.

CLASS VI.

The Levitation of Human Beings.

This has occurred in my presence on four occasions in darkness. The test conditions under which they took place were quite satisfactory, so far as the judgment was concerned; but ocular demonstration of such a fact is so necessary to disturb our pre-formed opinions as to "the naturally possible and impossible," that I will here only mention cases in which the deductions of reason were confirmed by the sense of sight.

On one occasion I witnessed a chair, with a lady sitting on it, rise several inches from the ground. On another occasion, to avoid the suspicion of this being in some way performed by herself, the lady knelt on the chair in such manner that its four feet were visible to us. It then rose about three inches, remained suspended for about ten seconds, and then slowly descended. At another time two children, on separate occasions, rose from the floor with their chairs, in full daylight, under (to me) most satisfactory conditions; for I was kneeling and keeping close watch upon the feet of the chair, and observing that no one might touch them.

The most striking cases of levitation which I have

witnessed have been with Mr. Home. On three separate occasions have I seen him raised completely from the floor of the room. Once sitting in an easy chair, once kneeling on his chair, and once standing up. On each occasion I had full opportunity of watching the occurrence as it was taking place.

There are at least a hundred recorded instances of Mr. Home's rising from the ground, in the presence of as many separate persons, and I have heard from the lips of the three witnesses to the most striking occurrence of this kind —the Earl of Dunraven, Lord Lindsay, and Captain C. Wynne—their own most minute accounts of what took place. To reject the recorded evidence on this subject is to reject all human testimony whatever; for no fact in sacred or profane history is supported by a stronger array of proofs.

The accumulated testimony establishing Mr. Home's levitations is overwhelming. It is greatly to be desired that some person, whose evidence would be accepted as conclusive by the scientific world—if indeed there lives a person whose testimony *in favour* of such phenomena would be taken—would seriously and patiently examine these alleged facts. Most of the eye-witnesses to these levitations are now living, and would, doubtless, be willing to give their evidence. But, in a few years, such *direct* evidence will be difficult, if not impossible, to be obtained.

Class VII.

Movement of Various Small Articles without Contact with any Person.

Under this heading I propose to describe some special phenomena which I have witnessed. I can do little more here than allude to some of the more striking facts, all of which, be it remembered, have occurred under circumstances that render trickery impossible. But it is idle to attribute these results to trickery, for I would again remind my readers that what I relate has not been accomplished at the house of a medium, but in my own house, where preparations have been quite impossible. A medium, walking into my dining-room, cannot, while seated in one part of the room with a number of persons keenly watching him, by trickery make an accordion play in *my own* hand when I hold it key downwards, or cause the same accordion to float about the room playing all the time. He cannot introduce machinery which will wave window-curtains or pull up Venetian blinds 8 feet off, tie a knot in a handker-chief and place it in a far corner of the room, sound notes on a distant piano, cause a card-plate to float about the room, raise a water-bottle and tumbler from the table, make a coral necklace rise on end, cause a fan to move about and fan the company, or set in motion a pendulum when enclosed in a glass case firmly cemented to the wall.

CLASS VIII.

Luminous Appearances.

These, being rather faint, generally require the room to be darkened. I need scarcely remind my readers again that, under these circumstances, I have taken proper pre-cautions to avoid being imposed upon by phosphorised oil, or other means. Moreover, many of these lights are such as I have tried to imitate artificially, but cannot.

Under the strictest test conditions, I have seen a solid self-luminous body, the size and nearly the shape of a turkey's egg, float noiselessly about the room, at one time higher than any one present could reach standing on tiptoe, and then gently descend to the floor. It was visible for more than ten minutes, and before it faded away it struck the table three times with a sound like that of a hard, solid body. During this time the medium was lying back, apparently insensible in an easy chair.

I have seen luminous points of light darting about and settling on the heads of different persons; I have had questions answered by the flashing of a bright light a desired number of times in front of my face. I have seen sparks of light rising from the table to the ceiling, and again falling upon the table, striking it with an audible sound. I have had an alphabetic communication given by luminous flashes occurring before me in the air, whilst my hand was moving about amongst them. I have seen a luminous cloud floating upwards to a picture. Under the strictest test conditions, I have more than once had a solid, self-luminous, crystalline body placed in my hand by a hand which did not belong to any person in the room. *In the light* I have seen a luminous cloud hover over a helio-trope on a side table, break a sprig off, and carry the sprig to a lady; and on some occasions I have seen a similar luminous cloud visibly condense to the form of a hand and carry small objects about. These, however, more properly belong to the next class of phenomena.

CLASS IX.

The Appearance of Hands, either Self-Luminous or Visible by Ordinary Light.

The forms of hands are frequently *felt* at dark *séances*, or under circumstances where they cannot be seen. More rarely I have *seen* the hands. I will here give no instances in which the phenomenon has occurred in darkness, but will simply select a few of the numerous instances in which I have seen the hands in the light.

A beautifully formed small hand rose up from an opening in a dining-table and gave me a flower; it appeared and then disappeared three times at intervals, affording me ample opportunity of satisfying myself that it was as real in appearance as my own. This occurred in the light in my own room, whilst I was holding the medium's hands and feet.

On another occasion a small hand and arm, like a baby's, appeared playing about a lady who was sitting next to me. It then passed to me and patted my arm and pulled my coat several times.

At another time a finger and thumb were seen to pick the petals from a flower in Mr. Home's button-hole, and lay them in front of several persons who were sitting near him.

A hand has repeatedly been seen by myself and others playing the keys of an accordion, both of the medium's hands being visible at the same time, and sometimes being held by those near him.

The hands and fingers do not always appear to me to be solid and life-like. Sometimes, indeed, they present more the appearance of a nebulous cloud partly condensed into the form of a hand. This is not equally visible to all present. For instance, a flower or other small object is seen to move; one person present will see a luminous cloud hovering over it, another will detect a nebulous-looking hand, whilst others will see nothing at all but the moving flower. I have more than once seen, first an object move, then a luminous cloud appear to form about it, and, lastly, the cloud condense into shape and become a perfectly-formed hand. At this stage, the hand is visible to all present. It is not always a mere form, but sometimes appears perfectly life-like and graceful, the fingers moving and the flesh apparently as human as that of any in the room. At the wrist, or arm, it becomes hazy, and fades off into a luminous cloud.

To the touch, the hand sometimes appears icy cold and dead, at other times, warm and life-like, grasping my own with the firm pressure of an old friend.

I have retained one of these hands in my own, firmly resolved not to let it escape. There was no struggle or effort made to get loose, but it gradually seemed to resolve itself into vapour, and faded in that manner from my grasp.

CLASS X.

Direct Writing.

This is the term employed to express writing which is not produced by any person present. I have had words and messages repeatedly written on privately-marked paper, under the most rigid test conditions, and have heard the pencil moving over the paper in the dark. The conditions —pre-arranged by myself—have been so strict as to be equally convincing to my mind as if I had seen the written characters formed. But as space will not allow me to enter into full particulars, I will merely select two instances in which my eyes as well as ears were witnesses to the operation.

The first instance which I shall give took place, it is true, at a dark *séance*, but the result was not less satisfactory on that account. I was sitting next to the medium, Miss Fox, the only other persons present being my wife and a lady relative, and I was holding the medium's two hands in one of mine, whilst her feet were resting on my feet. Paper was on the table before us, and my disengaged hand was holding a pencil.

A luminous hand came down from the upper part of the room, and after hovering near me for a few seconds, took the pencil from my hand, rapidly wrote on a sheet of paper, threw the pencil down, and then rose up over our heads, gradually fading into darkness.

My second instance may be considered the record of a failure. "A good failure often teaches more than the most successful experiment." It took place in the light, in my own room, with only a few private friends and Mr. Home present. Several circumstances, to which I need not further allude, had shown that the power that evening was strong. I therefore expressed a wish to witness the actual production of a written message such as I had heard described a short time before by a friend. Immediately an alphabetic communication was made as follows—"We will try." A pencil and some sheets of paper had been lying on the centre of the table; presently the pencil rose up on its point, and after advancing by hesitating jerks to the paper fell down.   It then rose and again fell.   A third time it tried, but with no better result.   After three unsuccessful attempts, a small wooden lath, which was lying near upon the table, slid towards the pencil, and rose a few inches from the table ; the pencil rose again, and propping itself against the lath, the two together made an effort to mark the paper.   It fell, and then a joint effort was again made.   After a third trial the lath gave it up and moved back to its place, the pencil lay as it fell across the paper, and an alphabetic message told us—"We have tried to do as you asked, but our power is exhausted."

CLASS XI.

Phantom Forms and Faces.

These are the rarest of the phenomena I have witnessed. The conditions requisite for their appearance appear to be so delicate, and such trifles interfere with their production, that only on very few occasions have I witnessed them under satisfactory test conditions.   I will mention two of these cases.

In the dusk of the evening, during a *séance* with Mr. Home at my house, the curtains of a window about eight feet from Mr. Home were seen to move.   A dark, shadowy, semi-transparent form, like that of a man, was then seen by all present standing near the window, waving the curtain with his hand.   As we looked, the form faded away and the curtains ceased to move.

The following is a still more striking instance.   As in the former case, Mr. Home was the medium.   A phantom form came from a corner of the room, took an accordion in its hand, and then glided about the room playing the instrument.   The form was visible to all present for many minutes, Mr. Home also being seen at the same time.   Coming rather close to a lady who was sitting apart from the rest of the company, she gave a slight cry, upon which it vanished.

CLASS XII.

Special Instances which seem to point to the Agency of an Exterior Intelligence.

It has already been shown that the phenomena are governed by an intelligence.   It becomes a question of importance as to the source of that intelligence.   Is it the

intelligence of the medium, of any of the other persons in
in the room, or is it an exterior intelligence? Without
wishing at present to speak positively on this point, I may
say that whilst I have observed many circumstances which
appear to show that the will and intelligence of the medium
have much to do with the phenomena,* I have observed
some circumstances which seem conclusively to point to the
agency of an outside intelligence, not belonging to any
human being in the room. Space does not allow me to
give here all the arguments which can be adduced to prove
these points, but I will briefly mention one or two circumstances out of many.

I have been present when several phenomena were going
on at the same time, some being unknown to the medium.
I have been with Miss Fox when she has been writing a
message automatically to one person present, whilst a message to another person on another subject was being given
alphabetically by means of "raps," and the whole time she
was conversing freely with a third person on a subject
totally different from either. Perhaps a more striking
instance is the following :—

During a *séance* with Mr. Home, a small lath, which I
have before mentioned, moved across the table to me, in the
light, and delivered a message to me by tapping my hand ;
I repeating the alphabet, and the lath tapping me at the
right letters. The other end of the lath was resting on the
table, some distance from Mr. Home's hands.

The taps were so sharp and clear, and the lath was
evidently so well under control of the invisible power which
was governing its movements, that I said, "Can the intelligence governing the motion of this lath change the
character of the movements, and give me a telegraphic
message through the Morse alphabet by taps on my hand?"
(I have every reason to believe that the Morse code was
quite unknown to any other person present, and it was only
imperfectly known to me). Immediately I said this, the
character of the taps changed, and the message was continued in the way I had requested. The letters were given
too rapidly for me to do more than catch a word here and
there, and consequently I lost the message; but I heard sufficient to convince me that there was a good Morse operator
at the other end of the line, wherever that might be.

---

* I do not wish my meaning to be misunderstood. What I mean is, *not*
that the medium's will and intelligence are actively employed in any conscious
or dishonest way in the production of the phenomena, but that they sometimes
appear to act in an unconscious manner.

Another instance. A lady was writing automatically by means of the planchette. I was trying to devise a means of proving that what she wrote was not due to "unconscious cerebration." The planchette, as it always does, insisted that, although it was moved by the hand and arm of the lady, the *intelligence* was that of an invisible being who was playing on her brain as on a musical instrument, and thus moving her muscles. I therefore said to this intelligence, "Can you see the contents of this room?" "Yes," wrote the planchette. "Can you see to read this newspaper?" said I, putting my finger on a copy of the *Times*, which was on a table behind me, but without looking at it. "Yes" was the reply of the planchette. "Well," I said, "if you can see that, write the word which is now covered by my finger, and I will believe you." The planchette commenced to move. Slowly and with great difficulty, the word "however" was written. I turned round and saw that the word "however" was covered by the tip of my finger.

I had purposely avoided looking at the newspaper when I tried this experiment, and it was impossible for the lady, had she tried, to have seen any of the printed words, for she was sitting at one table, and the paper was on another table behind, my body intervening.

CLASS XIII.

Miscellaneous Occurrences of a Complex Character.

Under this heading I propose to give several occurrences which cannot be otherwise classified owing to their complex character. Out of more than a dozen cases, I will select two. The first occurred in the presence of Miss Kate Fox. To render it intelligible, I must enter into some details.

Miss Fox had promised to give me a *séance* at my house one evening in the spring of last year. Whilst waiting for her, a lady relative, with my two eldest sons, aged fourteen and eleven, were sitting in the dining-room where the *séances* were always held, and I was sitting by myself, writing in the library. Hearing a cab drive up and the bell ring, I opened the door to Miss Fox, and took her directly into the dining-room. She said she would not go upstairs, as she could not stay very long, but laid her bonnet and shawl on a chair in the room. I then went to the dining-room door, and telling the two boys to go into the library and proceed with their lessons, I closed the door behind them, locked it, and (according to my usual custom at *séances*) put the key in my pocket.

We sat down, Miss Fox being on my right hand and the other lady on my left.   An Alphabetic message was soon given to turn the gas out, and we thereupon sat in total darkness, I holding Miss Fox's two hands in one of mine the whole time.   Very soon, a message was given in the following words, "We are going to bring something to show our power;" and almost immediately afterwards, we all heard the tinkling of a bell, not stationary, but moving about in all parts of the room: at one time by the wall, at another in a further corner of the room, now touching me on the head, and now tapping against the floor.   After ringing about the room in this manner for fully five minutes, it fell upon the table close to my hands.

During the time this was going on, no one moved and Miss Fox's hands were perfectly quiet.   I remarked that it could not be my little hand-bell which was ringing, for I left that in the library.   (Shortly before Miss Fox came, I had occasion to refer to a book, which was lying on a corner of a book-shelf.   The bell was on the book, and I put it on one side to get the book.   That little incident had impressed on my mind the fact of the bell being in the library.)   The gas was burning brightly in the hall outside the dining-room door, so that this could not be opened without letting light into the room, even had there been an accomplice in the house with a duplicate key, which there certainly was not.

I struck a light.   There, sure enough, was my own bell lying on the table before me.   I went straight into the library.   A glance showed that the bell was not where it ought to have been.   I said to my eldest boy, "Do you know where my little bell is?"   "Yes, papa," he replied, "there it is," pointing to where I had left it.   He looked up as he said this, and then continued, "No—it's not there, but it was there a little time ago."   "How do you mean?—has anyone come in and taken it?"   "No," said he, "no one has been in; but I am sure it was there, because when you sent us in here out of the dining-room, J. (the youngest boy) began ringing it so that I could no go on with my lessons, and I told him to stop."   J. corroborated this, and said that, after ringing it, he put the bell down where he had found it.

The second circumstance which I will relate occurred in the light, one Sunday evening, only Mr. Home and members of my family being present.   My wife and I had been spending the day in the country, and had brought home a few flowers we had gathered.   On reaching home, we gave them to a servant to put them in water.   Mr. Home came soon after, and we at once proceeded to the dining-room. As we were sitting down, a servant brought in the flowers which she had arranged in a vase. I placed it in the centre of the dining-table, which was without a cloth. This was the first time Mr. Home had seen these flowers.

After several phenomena had occurred, the conversation turned upon some circumstances which seemed only explicable on the assumption that matter had actually passed through a solid substance. Thereupon a message was given by means of the alphabet: " It is impossible for matter to pass through matter, but we will show you what we can do." We waited in silence. Presently a luminous appearance was seen hovering over the bouquet of flowers, and then, in full view of all present, a piece of china-grass 15 inches long, which formed the centre ornament of the bouquet, slowly rose from the other flowers, and then descended to the table in front of the vase between it and Mr. Home. It did not stop on reaching the table, but went straight through it, and we all watched it till it had entirely passed through. Immediately on the disappearance of the grass, my wife, who was sitting near Mr. Home, saw a hand come up from under the table between them, holding the piece of grass. It tapped her on the shoulder two or three times with a sound audible to all, then laid the grass on the floor, and disappeared. Only two persons saw the hand, but all in the room saw the piece of grass moving about as I have described. During the time this was taking place, Mr. Home's hands were seen by all to be quietly resting on the table in front of him. The place where the grass disappeared was 18 inches from his hands. The table was a telescope dining-table, opening with a screw ; there was no leaf in it, and the junction of the two sides formed a narrow crack down the middle. The grass had passed through this chink, which I measured, and found to be barely ⅛th inch wide. The stem of the piece of grass was far too thick to enable me to force it through this crack without injuring it, yet we had all seen it pass through quietly and smoothly ; and on examination, it did not show the slightest signs of pressure or abrasion.

THEORIES TO ACCOUNT FOR THE PHENOMENA OBSERVED.

First Theory.—The phenomena are all the results of tricks, clever mechanical arrangements, or legerdemain ; the mediums are impostors, and the rest of the company fools.

It is obvious that this theory can only account for a very small proportion of the facts observed. I am willing to

admit that some so-called mediums of whom the public
have heard much are arrant impostors who have taken
advantage of the public demand for spiritualistic excitement
to fill their purses with easily earned guineas ; whilst others
who have no pecuniary motive for imposture are tempted
to cheat, it would seem, solely by a desire for notoriety.   I
have met with several cases of imposture, some very ingenious, others so palpable, that no person who has witnessed the genuine phenomena could be taken in by them.
An inquirer into the subject finding one of these cases at
his first initiation is disgusted with what he detects at once
to be an imposture ; and he not unnaturally gives vent to
his feelings, privately or in print, by a sweeping denunciation
of the whole genus " medium."   Again with a thoroughly
genuine medium, the first phenomena which are observed
are generally slight movements of the table, and faint taps
under the medium's hands or feet.   These of course are
quite easy to be imitated by the medium, or anyone at the
table.   If, as sometimes occurs, nothing else takes place, the
sceptical observer goes away with the firm impression that
his superior acuteness detected cheating on the part of the
medium, who was consequently afraid to proceed with any
more tricks in *his* presence.   He, too, writes to the news-
papers exposing the whole imposture, and probably in-
dulges in moral sentiments about the sad spectacle of persons, apparently intelligent, being taken in by imposture
which he detected at once.

There is a wide difference between the tricks of a professional conjurer, surrounded by his apparatus, and aided
by any number of concealed assistants and confederates,
deceiving the senses by clever sleight of hand on his own
platform, and the phenomena occurring in the presence of
Mr. Home, which take place in the light, in a private room
that almost up to the commencement of the *séance* has
been occupied as a living room, and surrounded by private
friends of my own, who not only will not countenance the
slightest deception, but who are watching narrowly every
thing that takes place.   Moreover, Mr. Home has frequently
been searched before and after the *séances*, and he *always*
offers to allow it.   During the most remarkable occurrences
I have occasionally held both his hands, and placed my feet
on his feet.   On no single occasion have I proposed a modification of arrangements for the purpose of rendering trickery
less possible which he has not at once assented to, and
frequently he has himself drawn attention to tests which
might be tried.

I speak chiefly of Mr, Home, as he is so much more powerful than most of the other mediums I have experimented with. But with all I have taken such precautions as place trickery out of the list of possible explanations.

Be it remembered that an explanation to be of any value must satisfy *all* the conditions of the problem. It is not enough for a person, who has perhaps seen only a few of the inferior phenomena, to say "I suspect it was all cheating," or, "I saw how some of the tricks could be done."

Second Theory.—The persons at a *séance* are the victims of a sort of mania or delusion, and imagine phenomena to occur which have no real objective existence.

Third Theory.—The whole is the result of conscious or unconscious cerebral action.

These two theories are evidently incapable of embracing more than a small portion of the phenomena, and they are improbable explanations for even those. They may be dismissed very briefly.

I now approach the "Spiritual" theories. It must be remembered that the word "spirits" is used in a very vague sense by the generality of people.

Fourth Theory.—The result of the spirit of the medium, perhaps in association with the spirits of some or all of the people present.

Fifth Theory.—The actions of evil spirits or devils, personifying who or what they please, in order to undermine Christianity and ruin men's souls.

Sixth Theory.—The actions of a separate order of beings, living on this earth, but invisible and immaterial to us. Able, however, occasionally to manifest their presence. Known in almost all countries and ages as demons (not necessarily bad), gnomes, fairies, kobolds, elves, goblins, Puck, &c.

Seventh Theory.—The actions of departed human beings— the spiritual theory *par excellence.*

Eighth Theory.—*(The Psychic Force Theory).*—This is a necessary adjunct to the 4th, 5th, 6th, and 7th, theories rather than a theory by itself.

According to this theory the "medium," or the circle of people associated together as a whole, is supposed to possess a force, power, influence, virtue, or gift, by means of which intelligent beings are enabled to produce the phenomena observed. What these intelligent beings are, is a subject for other theories.

It is obvious that a "medium" possesses a *something* which is not possessed by an ordinary being. Give this *something* a name. Call it "*x*" if you like. Mr. Serjeant Cox calls it Psychic Force. There has been so much misunderstanding on this subject that I think it best to give the following explanation in Mr. Serjeant Cox's own words :—

"The Theory of *Psychic Force* is in itself merely the recognition of the now almost undisputed fact that under certain conditions, as yet but imperfectly ascertained, and within a limited, but as yet undefined, distance from the bodies of certain persons having a special nerve organisation, a Force operates by which, without muscular contact or connection, action at a distance is caused, and visible motions and audible sounds are produced in solid substances. As the presence of such an organisation is necessary to the phenomenon, it is reasonably concluded that the Force does, in some manner as yet unknown, proceed from that organisation. As the organism is itself moved and directed within its structure by a Force which either is, or is controlled by, the Soul, Spirit, or Mind (call it what we may) which constitutes the individual being we term 'the Man,' it is an equally reasonable conclusion that the Force which causes the motions beyond the limits of the body is the same Force that produces motion within the limits of the body. And, inasmuch as the external force is seen to be often directed by Intelligence, it is an equally reasonable conclusion that the directing Intelligence of the external force is the same Intelligence that directs the Force internally. This is the force to which the name of *Psychic Force* has been given by me as properly designating a force which I thus contend to be traced back to the Soul or Mind of the Man as its source. But I, and all who adopt this theory of Psychic Force as being the agent through which the phenomena are produced, do not thereby intend to assert that this Psychic Force may not be sometimes seized and directed by some other Intelligence than the Mind of the Psychic. The most ardent Spiritualists practically admit the existence of Psychic Force under the very inappropriate name of Magnetism (to which it has no affinity whatever), for they assert that the Spirits of the Dead can only do the acts attributed to them by using the Magnetism (that is, the Psychic Force) of the Medium. The difference between the advocates of Psychic Force and the Spiritualists consists in this—that we contend that there is as yet insufficient proof of any other directing agent than the Intelligence of the Medium, and no proof whatever of the agency of Spirits of the Dead ; while the Spiritualists hold it as a faith, not demanding further proof, that Spirits of the Dead are the sole agents in the production of all the phenomena. Thus the controversy resolves itself into a pure question of *fact*, only to be determined by a laborious and long-continued series of experiments and an extensive collection of psychological *facts*, which should be the first duty of the Psychological Society, the formation of which is now in progress."

MISS FLORENCE COOK'S MEDIUMSHIP.

[THE following letters appeared in the Spiritualistic journals at the dates which they bear. They form a fit conclusion to this series of papers] :—

SIR,—It has been my endeavour to keep as clear of controversy as possible, in writing or speaking about so inflammatory a topic as the phenomena called Spiritual. Except in very few cases, where the prominent position of my opponent would have caused my silence to be ascribed to other than the real motives, I have made no reply to the attacks and misrepresentations which my connection with this subject has entailed upon me.

The case is otherwise, however, when a few lines from me may perhaps assist in removing an unjust suspicion which is cast upon another. And when this other person is a woman,—young sensitive, and innocent,—it becomes especially a duty for me to give the weight of my testimony in favour of her whom I believe to be unjustly accused.

Among all the arguments brought forward on either side touching the phenomena of Miss Cook's mediumship, I see very few *facts* stated in such a way as to lead an unprejudiced reader, provided he can trust the judgment and veracity of the narrator, to say, "Here at last is absolute proof." I see plenty of strong assertion, much unintentional exaggeration, endless conjecture and supposition, no little insinuation of fraud, and some amount of vulgar buffoonery; but no one has come forward with a positive assertion, based upon the evidence of his own senses, to the effect that when the form which calls itself "Katie" is visible in the room, the body of Miss Cook is either actually in the cabinet or is not there.

It appears to me that the whole question narrows itself into this small compass. Let either of the above alternatives be proved to be a fact, and all the other collateral questions may be dismissed. But the proof must be absolute, and not based upon inferential reasoning, or assumed upon the supposed integrity of seals, knots, and sewing; for I have reason to know that the power at work in these phenomena, like Love, "laughs at locksmiths."

I was in hopes that some of those friends of Miss Cook, who have attended her *séances* almost from the commencement, and who appear to have been highly favoured in the tests they have received, would ere this, have borne testimony in her favour. In default, however, of evidence from those who have followed these phenomena from their beginning nearly three years ago, let me, who have only been admitted as it were, at the eleventh hour, state a circumstance which came under my notice at a *séance* to which I was invited by the favour of Miss Cook, a few days after the disgraceful occurrence which has given rise to this controversy.

The *séance* was held at the house of Mr. Luxmore, and the "cabinet" was a back drawing room, separated from the front room in which the company sat by a curtain.

The usual formality of searching the room and examining the fastenings having been gone through, Miss Cook entered the cabinet.

After a little time the form Katie appeared at the side of the curtain, but soon retreated, saying her medium was not well, and could not be put into a sufficiently deep sleep to make it safe for her to be left.

I was sitting within a few feet of the curtain close behind which Miss Cook was sitting, and I could frequently hear her moan and sob, as if in pain. This uneasiness continued at intervals nearly the whole duration of the *séance*, *and once, when the form of Katie was standing before me in the room, I distinctly heard a sobbing, moaning sound, identical with that which Miss Cook had been making at intervals the whole time of the séance, come from behind the curtain where the young lady was supposed to be sitting.*

I admit that the figure was startingly life-like and real, and, as far as I could see in the somewhat dim light, the features resembled those of Miss Cook; but still the positive evidence of one of my own senses that the moan came from Miss Cook in the cabinet, whilst the figure was outside, is too strong to be upset by a mere inference to the contrary, however well supported.

Your readers, sir, know me, and will, I hope, believe that I will not come hastily to an opinion, or ask them to agree with me on insufficient evidence. It is perhaps expecting too much to think that the little incident I have mentioned will have the same weight with them that it had with me.

But this I do beg of them—Let those who are inclined to judge Miss Cook harshly, suspend their judgment until I bring forward positive evidence which I think will be sufficient to settle the question.

Miss Cook is now devoting herself exclusively to a series of private *séances* with me and one or two friends. The *séances* will probably extend over some months, and I am promised that every desirable test shall be given to me. These *séances* have not been going on many weeks, but enough has taken place to thoroughly convince me of the perfect truth and honesty of Miss Cook, and to give me every reason to expect that the promises so freely made to me by Katie will be kept.

All I now ask is that your readers will not hastily assume that everything which is *primâ facie* suspicious necessarily implies deception, and that they will suspend their judgment until they hear from me again on this subject.—I am, &c.,

WILLIAM CROOKES.

20 MORNINGTON ROAD, LONDON,
February 3, 1874.

SPIRIT-FORMS.

IN a letter which I wrote to this journal early in February last, speaking of the phenomena of spirit-forms which have appeared through Miss Cook's mediumship, I said, " Let those who are inclined to judge Miss Cook harshly suspend their judgment until I bring forward positive evidence which I think will be sufficient to settle the question. Miss Cook is now devoting herself exclusively to a series of private *séances* with me and one or two friends. . . . Enough has taken place to thoroughly convince me of the perfect truth and honesty of Miss Cook, and to give me every reason to expect that the promises so freely made to me by Katie will be kept."

In that letter I described an incident which, to my mind, went very far towards convincing me that Katie and Miss Cook were two separate material beings. When Katie was outside the cabinet, standing before me, I heard a moaning noise from Miss Cook in the cabinet. I am happy to say that I have at last obtained the " absolute proof" to which I referred in the above-quoted letter.

I will, for the present, pass over most of the tests which

Katie has given me on the many occasions when Miss Cook has favoured me with *séances* at this house, and will only describe one or two which I have recently had. I have for some time past been experimenting with a phosphorus lamp, consisting of a 6-oz. or 8-oz. bottle, containing a little phosphorised oil, and tightly corked. I have had reason to hope that by the light of this lamp some of the mysterious phenomena of the cabinet might be rendered visible, and Katie has also expressed herself hopefully as to the same result.

On March 12th, during a *séance* here, after Katie had been walking amongst us and talking for some time, she retreated behind the curtain which separated my laboratory, where the company was sitting, from my library which did temporary duty as a cabinet. In a minute she came to the curtain and called me to her, saying, " Come into the room and lift my medium's head up, she has slipped down." Katie was then standing before me clothed in her usual white robes and turban head-dress. I immediately walked into the library up to Miss Cook, Katie stepping aside to allow me to pass. I found Miss Cook had slipped partially off the sofa, and her head was hanging in a very awkward position. I lifted her onto the sofa, and in so doing had satisfactory evidence, in spite of the darkness, that Miss Cook was not attired in the " Katie " costume, but had on her ordinary black velvet dress, and was in a deep trance. Not more than three seconds elapsed between my seeing the white-robed Katie standing before me and my raising Miss Cook on to the sofa from the position into which she had fallen.

On returning to my post of observation by the curtain, Katie again appeared, and said she thought she should be able to show herself and her medium to me at the same time. The gas was then turned out, and she asked for my phosphorus lamp. After exhibiting herself by it for some seconds, she handed it back to me, saying, " Now come in and see my medium." I closely followed her into the library, and by the light of my lamp saw Miss Cook lying on the sofa just as I had left her. I looked round for Katie, but she had disappeared. I called her, but there was no answer.

On resuming my place, Katie soon reappeared, and told me that she had been standing close to Miss Cook all the time. She then asked if she might try an experiment herself, and taking the phosphorus lamp from me she passed behind the curtain, asking me not to look in for the present.

In a few minutes she handed the lamp back to me, saying she could not succeed, as she had used up all the power, but would try again another time.   My eldest son, a lad of fourteen, who was sitting opposite me, in such a position that he could see behind the curtain, tells me he distinctly saw the phosphorus lamp apparently floating about in space over Miss Cook, illuminating her as she lay motionless on the sofa, but he could not see anyone holding the lamp.

I pass on to a *séance* held last night at Hackney.   Katie never appeared to greater perfection, and for nearly two hours she walked about the room, conversing familiarly with those present.   On several occasions she took my arm when walking, and the impression conveyed to my mind that it was a living woman by my side, instead of a visitor from the other world, was so strong that the temptation to repeat a recent celebrated experiment became almost irresistible.   Feeling, however, that if I had not a spirit, I had at all events a *lady* close to me, I asked her permission to clasp her in my arms, so as to be able to verify the interesting observations which a bold experimentalist has recently somewhat verbosely recorded.   Permission was graciously given, and I accordingly did—well, as any gentleman would do under the circumstances.   Mr. Volckman will be pleased to know that I can corroborate his statement that the "ghost" (not "struggling," however,) was as material a being as Miss Cook herself.   But the sequel shows how wrong it is for an experimentalist, however accurate his observations may be, to venture to draw an important conclusion from an insufficient amount of evidence.

Katie now said she thought she should be able this time to show herself and Miss Cook together.   I was to turn the gas out and then come with my phosphorus lamp into the room now used as a cabinet.   This I did, having previously asked a friend who was skilful at shorthand to take down any statement I might make when in the cabinet, knowing the importance attaching to first impressions, and not wishing to leave more to memory than necessary.   His notes are now before me.

I went cautiously into the room, it being dark, and felt about for Miss Cook.   I found her crouching on the floor. Kneeling down, I let air enter the lamp, and by its light I saw the young lady dressed in black velvet, as she had been in the early part of the evening, and to all appearance perfectly senseless ; she did not move when I took her hand and held the light quite close to her face, but continued quietly breathing. Raising the lamp, I looked around and saw Katie standing close behind Miss Cook. She was robed in flowing white drapery as we had seen her previously during the *séance.* Holding one of Miss Cook's hands in mine, and still kneeling, I passed the lamp up and down so as to illuminate Katie's whole figure and satisfy myself thoroughly that I was really looking at the veritable Katie whom I had clasped in my arms a few minutes before, and not at the phantasm of a disordered brain. She did not speak, but moved her head and smiled in recognition. Three separate times did I carefully examine Miss Cook crouching before me, to be sure that the hand I held was that of a living woman, and three separate times did I turn the lamp to Katie and examine her with steadfast scrutiny until I had no doubt whatever of her objective reality. At last Miss Cook moved slightly, and Katie instantly motioned me to go away. I went to another part of the cabinet and then ceased to see Katie, but did not leave the room till Miss Cook woke up, and two of the visitors came in with a light.

Before concluding this article I wish to give some of the points of difference which I have observed between Miss Cook and Katie. Katie's height varies; in my house I have seen her six inches taller than Miss Cook. Last night, with bare feet and not " tip-toeing," she was four and a half inches taller than Miss Cook. Katie's neck was bare last night; the skin was perfectly smooth both to touch and sight, whilst on Miss Cook's neck is a large blister, which under similar circumstances is distinctly visible and rough to the touch. Katie's ears are unpierced, whilst Miss Cook habitually wears earrings. Katie's complexion is very fair, while that of Miss Cook is very dark. Katie's fingers are much longer than Miss Cook's, and her face is also larger. In manners and ways of expression there are also many decided differences.

Miss Cook's health is not good enough to allow of her giving more of these test *séances* for the next few weeks, and we have, therefore, strongly advised her to take an entire rest before recommencing the experimental campaign which I have sketched out for her, and the results of which I hope to be able to record at some future day.

20 MORNINGTON ROAD, N.W.,
   March 30th, 1874.

THE LAST OF KATIE KING.

THE PHOTOGRAPHING OF KATIE KING BY THE AID OF THE ELECTRIC LIGHT.

HAVING taken a very prominent part of late at Miss Cook's *séances*, and having been very successful in taking numerous photographs of Katie King by the aid of the electric light, I have thought that the publication of a few of the details would be of interest to the readers of the *Spiritualist*.

During the week before Katie took her departure she gave *séances* at my house almost nightly, to enable me to photograph her by artificial light. Five complete sets of photographic apparatus were accordingly fitted up for the purpose, consisting of five cameras, one of the whole-plate size, one half-plate, one quarter-plate, and two binocular stereoscopic cameras, which were all brought to bear upon Katie at the same time on each occasion on which she stood for her portrait. Five sensitising and fixing baths were used, and plenty of plates were cleaned ready for use in advance, so that there might be no hitch or delay during the photographing operations, which were performed by myself, aided by one assistant.

My library was used as a dark cabinet. It has folding doors opening into the laboratory ; one of these doors was taken off its hinges, and a curtain suspended in its place to enable Katie to pass in and out easily. Those of our friends who were present were seated in the laboratory facing the curtain, and the cameras were placed a little behind them, ready to photograph Katie when she came outside, and to photograph anything also inside the cabinet, whenever the curtain was withdrawn for the purpose. Each evening there were three or four exposures of plates in the five cameras, giving at least fifteen separate pictures at each *séance ;* some of these were spoilt in the developing, and some in regulating the amount of light. Altogether I have forty-four negatives, some inferior, some indifferent, and some excellent.

Katie instructed all the sitters but myself to keep their seats and to keep conditions, but for some time past she has given me permission to do what I liked—to touch her, and to enter and leave the cabinet almost whenever I pleased. I have frequently followed her into the cabinet, and have sometimes seen her and her medium together, but most generally I have found nobody but the entranced medium lying on the floor, Katie and her white robes having instantaneously disappeared.

During the last six months Miss Cook has been a frequent visitor at my house, remaining sometimes a week at a time. She brings nothing with her but a little hand-bag, not locked; during the day she is constantly in the presence of Mrs. Crookes, myself, or some other member of my family, and, not sleeping by herself, there is absolutely no opportunity for any preparation even of a less elaborate character than would be required for enacting Katie King. I prepare and arrange my library myself as the dark cabinet, and usually, after Miss Cook has been dining and conversing with us, and scarcely out of our sight for a minute, she walks direct into the cabinet, and I, at her request, lock its second door, and keep possession of the key all through the *séance;* the gas is then turned out, and Miss Cook is left in darkness.

On entering the cabinet Miss Cook lies down upon the floor, with her head on a pillow, and is soon entranced. During the photographic *séances*, Katie muffled her medium's head up in a shawl to prevent the light falling upon her face. I frequently drew the curtain on one side when Katie was standing near, and it was a common thing for the seven or eight of us in the laboratory to see Miss Cook and Katie at the same time, under the full blaze of the electric light. We did not on these occasions actually see the face of the medium because of the shawl, but we saw her hands and feet; we saw her move uneasily under the influence of the intense light, and we heard her moan occasionally. I have one photograph of the two together, but Katie is seated in front of Miss Cook's head.

During the time I have taken an active part in these *séances* Katie's confidence in me gradually grew, until she refused to give a *séance* unless I took charge of the arrangements. She said she always wanted me to keep close to her, and near the cabinet, and I found that after this confidence was established, and she was satisfied I would not break any promise I might make to her, the phenomena increased greatly in power, and tests were freely given that would have been unobtainable had I approached the subject in another manner. She often consulted me about persons present at the *séances*, and where they should be placed, for of late she had become very nervous, in consequence of certain ill-advised suggestions that force should be employed as an adjunct to more scientific modes of research.

One of the most interesting of the pictures is one in which I am standing by the side of Katie; she has her bare foot upon a particular part of the floor. Afterwards I dressed Miss Cook like Katie, placed her and myself in exactly the same position, and we were photographed by the same cameras, placed exactly as in the other experiment, and illuminated by the same light. When these two pictures are placed over each other, the two photographs of myself coincide exactly as regards stature, &c., but Katie is half a head taller than Miss Cook, and looks a big woman in comparison with her. In the breadth of her face, in many of the pictures, she differs essentially in size from her medium, and the photographs show several other points of difference.

But photography is as inadequate to depict the perfect beauty of Katie's face, as words are powerless to describe her charms of manner. Photography may, indeed, give a map of her countenance ; but how can it reproduce the brilliant purity of her complexion, or the ever-varying expression of her most mobile features, now overshadowed with sadness when relating some of the bitter experiences of her past life, now smiling with all the innocence of happy girlhood when she had collected my children round her, and was amusing them by recounting anecdotes of her adventures in India?

> " Round her she made an atmosphere of life;
>   The very air seemed lighter from her eyes,
> They were so soft and beautiful, and rife
>   With all we can imagine of the skies;
> Her overpowering presence make you feel
> It would not be be idolatry to kneel."

Having seen so much of Katie lately, when she has been illuminated by the electric light, I am enabled to add to the points of difference between her and her medium which I mentioned in a former article. I have the most absolute certainty that Miss Cook and Katie are two separate individuals so far as their bodies are concerned. Several little marks on Miss Cook's face are absent on Katie's. Miss Cook's hair is so dark a brown as almost to appear black; a lock of Katie's which is now before me, and which she allowed me to cut from her luxuriant tresses, having first traced it up to the scalp and satisfied myself that it actually grew there, is a rich golden auburn.

On one evening I timed Katie's pulse. It beat steadily at 75, whilst Miss Cook's pulse a little time after, was going at its usual rate of 90. On applying my ear to Katie's chest I could hear a heart beating rythmically inside, and pulsating even more steadily than did Miss Cook's heart when she allowed me to try a similar experiment after the *séance.*

Tested in the same way Katie's lungs were found to be sounder than her medium's, for at the time I tried my experiment Miss Cook was under medical treatment for a severe cough.

Your readers may be interested in having Mrs. Ross Church's, and your own accounts of the last appearance of Katie, supplemented by my own narrative, as far as I can publish it. When the time came for Katie to take her farewell I asked' that she would let me see the last of her. Accordingly when she had called each of the company up to her and had spoken to them a few words in private, she gave some general directions for the future guidance and protection of Miss Cook. From these, which were taken down in shorthand, I quote the following: "Mr. Crookes has done very well throughout, and I leave Florrie with the greatest confidence in his hands, feeling perfectly sure he will not abuse the trust I place in him. He can act in any emergency better than I can myself, for he has more strength." Having concluded her directions, Katie invited me into the cabinet with her, and allowed me to remain there to the end.

After closing the curtain she conversed with me for some time, and then walked across the room to where Miss Cook was lying senseless on the floor. Stooping over her, Katie touched her, and said, "Wake up, Florrie, wake up! I must leave you now." Miss Cook then woke and tearfully entreated Katie to stay a little time longer. "My dear, I can't; my work is done. God bless you," Katie replied, and then continued speaking to Miss Cook. For several minutes the two were conversing with each other, till at last Miss Cook's tears prevented her speaking. Following Katie's instructions I then came forward to support Miss Cook, who was falling on to the floor, sobbing hysterically. I looked round, but the white-robed Katie had gone. As soon as Miss Cook was sufficiently calmed, a light was procured and I led her out of the cabinet.

The almost daily *séances* with which Miss Cook has lately favoured me have proved a severe tax upon her strength, and I wish to make the most public acknowledgment of the obligations I am under to her for her readiness to assist me in my experiments. Every test that I have proposed she has at once agreed to submit to with the utmost willingness ; she is open and straightforward in speech, and I have never seen anything approaching the slightest symptom of a wish to deceive. Indeed, I do not believe she could carry on a deception if she were to try, and if she did she would certainly be found out very quickly, for such a line of action is altogether foreign to her nature. And to imagine that an innocent school-girl of fifteen should be able to conceive and then successfully carry out for three years so gigantic an imposture as this, and in that time should submit to any test which might be imposed upon her, should bear the strictest scrutiny, should be willing to be searched at any time, either before or after a *séance*, and should meet with even better success in my own house than at that of her parents, knowing that she visited me with the express object of submitting to strict scientific tests,—to imagine, I say, the Katie King of the last three years to be the result of imposture does more violence to one's reason and common sense than to believe her to be what she herself affirms.

It would not be right for me to conclude this article without also thanking Mr. and Mrs. Cook for the great facilities they have given me to carry on these observations and experiments.

My thanks and those of all Spiritualists are also due to Mr. Charles Blackburn for the generous manner in which he has made it possible for Miss Cook to devote her whole time to the development of these manifestations and latterly o their scientific examination.

GLASGOW:
H. NISBET, PRINTER AND STEREOTYPER,
219 GEORGE STREET.